My Dyslexic Life

A Journey Out of the Shadows

SCOTT DOUTHIT

Robert D. Reed Publishers · Bandon, OR

Robert D. Reed Publishers
P.O. Box 1992
Bandon, OR 97411
Phone: 541-347-9882; Fax: -9883
E-mail: 4bobreed@msn.com
Website: www.rdrpublishers.com

Editor: Rodrigo A. Munoz, Ralph Scott, and Cleone Reed
Designer: Amy Cole
Cover: Rodrigo A. Munoz
Cover photo: Dreamstime ID 2591459 / invisioncare.com

Soft Cover ISBN: 978-1-944297-60-2
EBook ISBN: 978-1-944297-61-9

Library of Congress Control Number: 2020931240

Designed and Formatted in the United States of America

To my mother
Florence Douthit

ACKNOWLEDGMENTS

T he heart and soul of this book could not have been achieved without the constant love and support of my one true love Lynn, who I will always love because with her I have been able to be myself and be loved for it.

To my agent Claire Lazar-Lemus, who has been my anchor and pushed and guided me to do my very best. She joined me on this journey without hesitation, and for that I am forever grateful.

To my editor Rodrigo A. Munoz, for your expertise and input. You are exceptional at what you do.

Writing this book was an emotional journey, and I would like to thank all those who believed and encouraged me along the way: Lauren Douthit, Stephen Douthit, Sally Cotton, Russ Smith, Zachary Adamis, Claudia Koochek, and all my former students who told me I should put my stories in a book.

Contents

PROLOGUE

The hardest thing about being dyslexic is the self-doubt. I am in my 60s and a professional educator, but it doesn't take much to make me wonder if maybe they were right: maybe I *am* a fake, a liar, and a fraud. It's easy for others to judge... but believing in myself fully and sincerely is the hard part for me.

When I was a child, *The Wizard of Oz* had a tremendous impact on me. Not because the Wicked Witch scared the poop out of me (which she did), and not even because flying monkeys were cool (although they were). No, *The Wizard of Oz* had a profound effect on me because of the Wizard himself. I always identified with the Wizard because he could perform amazing magic tricks and fool people into believing that he had great powers, but if anybody ever peeked behind the curtain, they would discover the truth: a little man with no magical powers whatsoever. A fake, a fraud, a phony.

Even after becoming an adult, no matter how important my job was or how much money I made, I was always worried that one day somebody would look behind my curtain and find out who I really was.

I have spent my entire life trying to be who I am now. This is my journey, and for the first time in my life, I am coming Out of the Shadows.

I am what I am... Life's not worth a damn,
'til you can say, "Hey world, I am what I am."
— La Cage Aux Folles

These are my memories of growing up with dyslexia, but I've written this book for *everyone* who doesn't understand why they cannot do what others can do. I've written this book for *everyone* who believes they are the only ones who don't belong and yet don't know why.

1.

THE JOURNEY BEGINS

The day that I had been anticipating and dreading had finally arrived. This wasn't my first opening night as a director of musical theater, but I still had butterflies in my stomach and a head full of self-doubt.

Did I prepare the kids enough?

Did I cast the play properly?

Did I even pick the right play?

"Stop it, Scott, STOP IT!" I thought. Every year I do this to myself.

For more than twenty years, I've directed our middle school musical at Charles Armstrong School. I started the program with ten students performing in our school's multipurpose room; it has since blossomed into a production involving more than a hundred and twenty actors performing off-campus to sold-out crowds in a five-hundred-seat professional theater. But every year, this point is the hardest part of the journey for me. Although I would prefer to skip the worrying, I can't do anything but wait the few hours with the actors until we take the bus to the theater.

As I stand before the red double doors to the school's multipurpose room, I prepare myself for the frenzied anticipation that is about to surround me. Entering, I am immediately besieged by each young actor's frantic questions. I guess I'm not the only one feeling afraid... but I can't let on.

"What do I do if I can't remember my lines during the play, Mr. D?" Mary asks. Her face is pale as a ghost, her fingers twiddling faster than a looping roller coaster as she nervously paces back and forth, hitting her rolled-up script against her glistening palm.

"Have faith in the work that you've put in," I respond.

"Mr. D! Mr. D!" calls Jane, darting from the music room like a minnow chased by a hungry fish. Tugging on my shirt, her face only inches from mine, she pleads, "What scenes am I in? I can't remember!"

After several "Don't worry" reassurances, a few "Here are your scenes" reminders, and lots of encouragement to "Relax and have fun with it," the cast settles down. They break into small groups, some to rehearse lines while others practice their dances. Some sit alone in silence; some, script in hand, talk to themselves.

Off in the corner, two eighth grade students are engaged in conversation. One of the two, Grace, was in my PE class. Grace was unique; she didn't indulge in applying makeup or become self-consumed by the latest trends. Her golden skin reflected the sun-kissed bleached streaks in her long, tangled hair. Sometimes, her messy hair hid her bold, blue, weary eyes. Those eyes never really looked happy, and often seemed filled with sadness and anxiety. They gently flickered, like a candle barely keeping alive. She hid her sorrow well, though, and the young boys flocked to her. She was tall, blonde, athletic, and

4

acted as if her life was perfect in every way. She was a middle school boy magnet.

Then there was James. James screamed energy! Nothing about him was calm or relaxing. He was the kid who was constantly moving around, doing jumping jacks, flicking rubber bands, and trying to be best friends with everyone he met. He was confident and proud to be himself. His fiery, kinked, orange hair stood tall as though reaching for the sun. Any obstacle in his life was nothing more than an accepted challenge.

"Do you have any brothers or sisters, James?" Grace asks.

"Yeah, I have a twin sister."

"You have a twin? Cool. Is she dyslexic too?"

"Nope."

"Good! She got lucky."

"What do you mean?"

"I hate being dyslexic!"

"Really? I kinda love being dyslexic. All my strengths come from it—y'know, like my creativity, ability to think outside of the box, and my imagination."

"Well, that's all well and good right now, because our school is just for dyslexic learners. But we're all in a bubble here. We can talk about our strengths and weaknesses and our different learning styles and feel safe here because we're all on the same side." Grace pauses and looks around to make sure none of the other students are listening to their conversation. "But outside, back home in the real world, I'm still dumb. I'm still treated like that stupid kid."

"Don't listen to them, Grace. You need to believe and have faith in yourself."

Grace laughs. "Are you for real? Can you even hear yourself? All that self-help crap works here at our school, but not out there. You can tell me to 'believe in myself' all you want," she scoffs, complete with mocking air quotes, "but that doesn't change how the world sees me."

Realizing that I've overheard them, James turns to me. "What do you think, Mr. D? You're dyslexic."

"I think that the crap I had to deal with fifty years ago is the same crap you two have to deal with right now. But in my opinion, the point is not that you're dyslexic; it's how you use it."

"What do you mean?" Grace asks.

"Everybody has to deal with being judged for something that they have no control over. That can be anything from the color of your skin, to the country you were born in, to the language that you speak. It's how you deal with it that matters."

"How would you know, Mr. D?" Grace demands. "You're this great teacher with all these awards. You've graduated from college, written plays, you're loved by everybody. If someone judges you for anything, you can ignore them or just laugh in their face. You know you're smart. Not me—when I go back to my neighborhood and my local school, I'll be going back to being that stupid kid again! You just don't know what it feels like."

I think for a moment... my mind going back in time...

"Hey retard! What are you reading?" Sammy asked, his inquiry stained with sarcasm.

"Sammy, you know this kid can't read. He's dumb as mud!" said Tommy.

I tried to ignore these taunts and continued to pretend to read my library book, *Robin Hood*.

"Tommy, he's so stupid he can't even talk, or maybe he's chicken. Scotty's afraid to talk because he stu...stu...stutters." Both boys laughed. I really hated being laughed at.

"Look, I think he's going to cry!" Tommy's taunt ripped into me. I strained, trying not to fulfill his prediction. "We're sorry, Scotty. We won't tell anybody that you can't read."

He didn't need to fake the sincerity; his snickering gave him away. "Hey everybody!" he yelled to the room full of children around us. "This kid is ten years old and can't read and he is sitting here pretending to read. What is he even doing in a library? You should be in the Kiddies' Section, Scotty, where all the books have pictures!"

Finally, from behind the Reference Desk, a woman adorned with those quintessential librarian glasses shot a "Shhhhh!" across the floor.

Their last insults still echoing in my ears, the boys ran laughing from the library, leaving me sitting there with everyone staring at me.

"Grace, I do know how you feel." I take a seat on the floor beside the two. "We have time before we leave for the theater. Let me tell you a little bit about myself that you may not already know."

2.

Paste and Stuff

In many ways, I was just like any other kid. I played in the dirt. I teased the family cat. I never wanted to go to bed at the appointed time. I fit in with my family. I was an older brother and the first son.

Life was good. I was good.

My mom talked about this grand place she intended to enroll me, a place called preschool that had jelly jars filled with colored pencils and paintbrushes, construction paper and safety scissors, fish tanks brimming with fish, swing sets and play structures, and—most importantly—lots of new friends. We did a lot of fun stuff at home, but making new friends? That seemed like a good idea, especially since I didn't have any real friends in the first place.

Don't get me wrong, I had a lot of friends. They just happened to be imaginary. There was Joe from a distant planet, who was strong and brave; Bruce the trickster, who was always trying to get me into trouble; and Mary, my favorite imaginary friend who I trusted with all my darkest secrets. But an actual human friend? Now that was different, and it seemed like a pretty good idea. And if preschool was as circus-like as Mom assured me, then I was all for it and ready to go. In fact, I remember I couldn't wait to zip up my new sunny orange backpack.

About two weeks later, the first day of preschool was finally here! As my mom drove me to school in our old blue Ford station wagon, I gazed out the smudged car window at the leaf-less trees whizzing by. I thought about the rainbow of pencils and construction paper, and in my mind's eye, I traced the path of goldfish as they raced around the tank. When we arrived at my new school, I jumped out of the car eager to start my first day. As I dragged my mom by the hand towards the entrance of the school, she stopped and knelt down. She placed her hands on my shoulders and looked me in the eyes.

"Are you nervous about leaving home for the first time?"

"No," I answered. Why should I be nervous? Preschool sounded like fun, I thought.

And it was... at first. All the paste you could eat, bugs to play with, my imaginary friends always at my side, and even, once in a while, actually talking to somebody real.

About a week into the school year, I met Susie Johnson. Under her frizzy red hair topped with a large blue polka-dotted bow, she beamed the biggest smile I'd ever seen outside of that picture of the Cheshire Cat in Mom's copy of *Alice's Adventures in Wonderland*. We liked to do the same things: playing outside, building forts, having imaginary battles against imaginary ene-mies. So far, preschool was great—everything I had hoped for. But one day it all changed. One day, it rained.

At home when it would rain, my sister and I went outside and played in the rain, splashing in puddles and getting all wet and muddy. When we were done, my mom would make us take a nice hot bath. I loved rainy days when I was at home. So, when the first rainy day occurred at preschool, I got up from the individual carpet where I'd been assembling a Lincoln Log tower and went directly outside to continue my play. Seemingly out of nowhere, the teacher stood towering above me. "Scotty, we don't play in the rain at preschool. We go inside where it's nice and dry."

Inside? What was the fun of going inside when you could play outside in the rain? So I asked why, and stated emphatically, "But it's fun outside!"

Covering the top of her head with a notebook to protect herself from the raindrops, the teacher knelt down, looked me directly in the eyes, and said, "Because I said so. That's why."

"Because!" Because? *Just* "because?" No explanation, no reason? When my mother said no to something, she always provided an explanation. "Don't play in the street because you could be hit by a bus. The bus is bigger than you and the bus will win, and you will lose. You will become a speed bump. Do you want to be a speed bump?" I would think about this scenario for a second or two and conclude that I positively wouldn't want to be a speed bump, that maybe my mother was right, and therefore I shouldn't play in the street. So, to have a person say "no" to me with "because" provided as the only (non)explanation was a completely foreign concept. This way of thinking was totally new to me, but Mom wasn't there, so what was I to do?

I came inside and dried off. I looked around to see what everyone else was doing, although I couldn't figure out what I would do here inside the classroom that would be better than playing in the rain. Some kids were coloring, which looked like fun until I noticed that the teacher kept asking them to color the pictures inside the lines. Inside the lines? This was another new concept. What was the fun in that? I always thought the lines were just to give you an idea of all the cool possibilities. Well, Miss Swanson might know something about rain, but I knew a little something about coloring. I decided to give it a try—my way.

I took a seat at the end of the table with the other kids, picked up a red Crayola, and applied it to the outline of a cowboy on a horse. Only I applied it to all that free and lovely white space outside the cowboy and the horse, making my own pictures using my imagination. My teacher must have been watching. Within the space of a minute, she came over and touched my hand, moving my crayon back inside the lines of the picture.

"The lines of the picture are for you to stay inside of," the teacher said sweetly. "You are supposed to color inside the lines, not outside."

Well, that didn't sound right. Was this like the rain all over again? "Why?" I asked.

She looked down at me, still smiling, but with something less warm in her eyes. "Because I said so, that's why." Then she turned and left, praising another student who was coloring the same picture... inside the lines.

So began the trend of "Because I said so." Guess preschool was going to be harder than I thought.

The next day when I returned to preschool I felt nervous and apprehensive, especially because it was still raining and I didn't know what to expect this time. I knew I couldn't go outside and play in the rain. Why? "Because I said so." I also knew I couldn't color outside the lines. Why? "Because I said so." So, what could I do where I could think up stuff and have some fun?

I looked around the room and saw that girl Susie, who was very nice to me the day before. She was doing something at a table that looked kind of interesting. I walked over, sat down next to her, and asked, "What's ya doin'?"

She looked up at me, smiled, and said, "I'm building a puzzle; do you want to help me?"

"Sure."

I always had fun playing with Susie because we always used our imaginations. I thought building a puzzle would be fun even though I had never built one before. It was my first time trying to solve a real problem. I looked at Susie and asked her, "What are we supposed to do?"

"You match up the pieces of the puzzle and put them together to make this picture," she said, holding up the top of the puzzle box. It had a picture of two horses running in a field. I looked at the picture and then at the table covered with hundreds of different pieces all mixed up. Who came up with this crazy idea? How was I supposed to make sense out of this? Some crazy diabolical madman had made a perfectly nice picture and then cut it into hundreds of jagged little pieces. Susie was assembling the nostrils and making it look easy, but the jumbled mound of puzzle pieces still looked intimidating to me.

Trying not to show my worry—I mean, after all, Susie could do it—I picked up some pieces and moved them around with my hand. But nothing seemed to fit. I started putting them together the only way that made any sense to me: by using brute force. Problem solved!

Susie was too preoccupied building her part of our puzzle to even notice what I was doing. After maybe ten minutes, I must have put together about fifteen pieces. Even though the outcome didn't look like two horses running through a field, I was proud of myself. I'd made something entirely different than just an image on a box top. I was putting together the puzzle my way.

"Hey Susie, look what I've done!" I said proudly, gesturing toward my creation.

"What have you done? This doesn't look like the picture on the box! Scotty, you can't just force pieces together. They have to fit together like mine," she said, pointing to the puzzle in front of her.

I was confused once again. I thought Susie had told me I could *build* a puzzle, not *fit* a puzzle. Susie seemed to know where every piece fit. To me, all these scattered puzzle pieces just looked like the Picasso painting Miss Swanson had showed us during our last art class: the nose on one side of the face, the mouth on the forehead, and the chin where the mouth was supposed to be. I couldn't make sense out of any of the pieces. They kept moving around in my head.

Susie looked at me and asked, "What's wrong? Don't you like making puzzles?"

I thought about it and said, "No, I'd rather eat paste."

"Why don't you like making puzzles?" she asked me. I told her that I didn't understand what I was supposed to do. How were all these little pieces supposed to make any sense? I couldn't figure out how hundreds of little jagged cardboard pieces were supposed to somehow transform into a beautiful picture.

She looked at me, very confused. "Why, any dummy can make a puzzle. Even my little sister could do *this* puzzle," she said.

Wait a second—did Susie just call me a dummy because I didn't understand this puzzle? I wasn't sure what was happening, but to my horror Susie called the teacher over to our table. "Miss Swanson! Miss Swanson!"

13

What happened next changed my life forever. When Miss Swanson walked up to our table, Susie opened her mouth and said, "I think there's something wrong with Scotty. He did this puzzle all wrong and I don't think he is really trying." She turned to me and crossed her arms. "He is ruining my puzzle and he's doing it on purpose."

What? Doing it on *purpose?* I didn't even know how to make a puzzle in the first place. Wait a second, I thought—isn't that why I'm here, to learn how to do this stuff? What's wrong with Susie? Why doesn't she like me? It's just a stupid puzzle and I thought she was my friend.

The teacher told her, "Give Scotty a little time. He'll get it."

"*Yeah,*" I thought, "*give me a little time and I'll show you, you big bag of snot.*"

Three rainy days later, I had connected six pieces together, three by force. Picasso had nothing on me. When "old snot bags" came over and saw my six puzzle pieces, she laughed and said, loud enough for all the other kids to hear, "Hey guys, look at this. Scotty can't even make a puzzle; he must be retarded."

Now, I wasn't certain what "retarded" meant, but I was pretty sure it wasn't good. All the kids began laughing at me, and this made me want to disappear.

That night when my dad got home from work, I asked him what "retarded" meant. He looked at me and said flatly, "Oh, being retarded means you don't have a brain. You know, like the scarecrow from *The Wizard of Oz*." And then he went back to reading his paper.

So here was another puzzle for me to solve. Why did the kids at school think I didn't have a brain? Was it because I couldn't put together that stupid puzzle? I didn't know the answer or have a clue how to solve this problem, but I did know one thing: I didn't like being laughed at.

I had no idea that this singular event was going to be the backstory of my life for the next sixty years.

"I have a question, Mr. D," James asked. "What's a 'back-story?' Is it different from a 'front-story?'" He smiled, laughing at his own joke.

"A backstory is your history," I explained. "It's what makes you who you are. You two are actors. When you get a character to play, you need to find the character's motivation, right? And how do you do that?"

"I know," Grace jumped in. "By finding the character's history—and if it's not in the script, you tell us to make it up. Like the show we're doing now; I'm playing an orphan, so I had to make up why I became an orphan, why my parents gave me up. That way I can play my character with conviction, because I know where she came from."

I nodded. "Exactly, and that's why I'm telling you these stories: so you can see my history."

"Oh, I get it!" James had that "Eureka!" look in his eyes. "So, did things get any better for you after preschool?"

3.

A Brand New Start

My parents, both newspaper reporters, were always trying to find the perfect community where they could both work and raise a family. They found that ideal location just as I was starting first grade, and we moved from Southern California to Berkeley. This move gave me an opportunity to start over in a brand new school, Oxford Elementary, along with a new neighborhood and, hopefully, the chance to meet new friends.

At first, things went well. I did meet new friends, and I liked Oxford Elementary. Although I was behind the other students in my schoolwork, I did okay in the classroom, and the teacher attributed my lagging to having just started out in a new school in a new town. She assured me I'd come along soon enough. As the school year progressed, I started to feel more comfortable with the other kids. Heck, I even forgot about the puzzle incident from preschool.

Like kids worldwide, all my new classmates loved recess. Every time the bell rang, they ran outside and broke into organized activities like dodgeball, hopscotch, and tetherball. It seemed almost like magic to me, because everybody knew exactly what group they belonged to and how to play.

On the first day of recess I ran outside too. Red rubber balls were bouncing, kids were screaming, jump ropes were slapping the ground. I eagerly stood near the swings watching some kids play four-square. I didn't know how to play, but the game seemed intense and exciting, and I was hoping that one of the kids would notice me and ask me to join. But that never happened, so I stood there alone as an outsider looking in.

On the second day of recess I ventured to a different section of the schoolyard. I cautiously stood behind the line near the tetherball courts, watching in awe at how fast the ball spun around the pole. When several of the kids walked toward me, my heart beat faster. Maybe this time someone would show me how to play. But that never happened. I stood there staring at the intricacies of the game alone, as if I existed to no one.

On the third day I sat on a bench near Mary and Kathy playing hopscotch. I didn't know how to play that game either. So there I sat.

Time moved slowly during recess, and I wasn't sure what was worse: being lost academically in the classroom, or lonely during recess. I guess the other kids were having so much fun they never even noticed me standing alone.

Because there was no place to go during recess to learn how to play these games, I finally gave up and decided to rely on my three longtime playmates: Me, Myself, and I. My imagination had always been my best friend anyway, so I started moving to the periphery of the recess area and into the Shadows. The Shadows were an imaginary place in my head where I felt safe, and where I was comfortable enough to be myself. So thereafter, during recess time, I would find a small corner of the schoolyard to play in away from the other children.

One day during recess I came across a bee on the ground. It wasn't moving. Because the bee appeared to be dead, it couldn't sting me. Bees sting and then they die, right? This one was dead, so he must have already used his stinger. Having reasoned this out, I decided to conduct a series of scientific experiments on Mr. Bee. Things were going quite well until I discovered something very odd. Apparently, Mr. Bee still had his stinger—and when I touched it, I got stung. It turns out that dead bees can still sting. Who knew? Not me, certainly. And boy, did it hurt!

I started screaming as my finger began to swell. I ran to the nearest teacher, hollering at the top of my lungs: "I've been stung! I've been stung! I was attacked by a swarm of vicious bees!"

I was pretty sure the teacher thought I was dying, and she immediately rushed me to the nurse's office. The nurse looked at my finger and said, "You have been stung by a bee." Looking back on it now, I do think this is where my dramatic side started kicking in.

"I know that," I told her. Where do they get these people from? Couldn't she tell I was in great pain and distress? Maybe I needed to go to the hospital—*stat*. I wasn't sure the nurse fully understood the gravity of this situation, because instead of rushing me to the emergency room, she asked me what I was doing when I got stung.

"I was playing," I said, becoming more agitated. I could feel my impatience building to a fever pitch.

Then she asked me, "Who were you playing with? Did they see the bee sting you?"

What? *"Does she have time for this line of questioning?"* I wondered. I mean, how much time did I have left before I died?

I decided I had better play along with her because she held my life in her antiseptic hands.

"I was playing with Mr. Bee and he stung me."

She looked horrified. "You were playing with a live bee? Weren't you scared?"

"The bee I was playing with was already dead," I told her. Now her look of horror turned to one that I recalled from my days in preschool: faintly disgusted, troubled, and a little bit pitying. Then she asked me a question that I had also heard before.

"Are you stupid or just retarded? Only an idiot would play with dead bees. I'm calling your mother to come pick you up." As she was leaving, the nurse turned back to add, "Maybe this is not the right school for you."

When my mom picked me up, we went out for ice cream and talked about what had transpired. She told me that I was normal, with a very active imagination, and that one day this imagination of mine would take me far. But for now, some people, like the school nurse, just didn't understand kids like me.

My mom got me. She understood, which made me feel good about myself, and that was good enough for me... until second grade.

"I can't believe that the school nurse called you stupid and retarded!" James was practically beside himself.

"I can't believe that you played with a dead bee. Weren't you worried that the other kids would think you were weird?" Grace said. "I thought you were trying to fit in at your new school."

"People seem to think that all kids are born knowing how to play recess games," I said. "I was not, so I used the one thing that worked for me: my imagination. I made up my own games."

James got excited. "Is that why you make up your own games for us in PE? In elementary school I loved playing those games you made up, like 'Star Wars' and 'Lord of the Rings.' They were always my favorites."

Barely able to hold back her annoyance, Grace asked, "Why didn't you just learn how to play kickball and fit in with all the other kids? Using your imagination at school just made you look different and stand out."

"Well, I got news for you: the schoolyard wasn't the only place I stood out."

A, B, C, Simple
as 1, 2, 3

When I was younger, I had a recurring dream about running a race where everyone was moving at normal speed except for me. I was running in slow motion, and everyone else dashed right past me—I just couldn't keep up. It was like I was struggling through quicksand while all the other kids were sprinting on a normal road.

This was exactly how second grade felt to me.

At first everything was okay. I had made new friends in school and I started to feel like I was a member of a group, and that I finally fit in. But something strange was happening to me in the classroom. No matter how hard I tried to understand what appeared before me, I couldn't really tell what the teacher was writing on the board. She would write a word and the letters would jump around. Sometimes, what I saw wasn't even what she actually wrote down. This happened with numbers, too. In fact, numbers were the worst: "21" appeared as "12" or "13" would look like "31"—and that was if I was lucky. Sometimes the numbers appeared to be floating in midair, moving around like they were alive.

"Boys and girls, please copy these numbers off the board," Miss White said to the class. Walking around the classroom to check everyone's work, she stopped by my desk to frown down at my paper. "Scotty, I wrote 13, not 31, and 24, not 42. Just look at the board and copy exactly what I wrote."

"But I did, Miss White! I did copy what's on the board!" I held up my paper as if this could prove my point, looking between it and the board in confusion.

"Why can't you do it right? You're not really trying, are you? Are you even paying attention?"

These comments hit me every day, but I wasn't sure what the teacher meant by them. Why couldn't I do anything right? If she didn't think I was really trying, what did she think I was doing? And then there was that one, most wicked question: "Are you paying attention?" Of course I was paying attention! Even though I wasn't always sure just what I was supposed to be paying attention to.

The harder I tried, the worse my situation seemed to become. The worse it became, the more frustrated my teacher would get. The more personal contact and communication I had with my teacher, the more agitated and angry she would become with me. I really had no idea what I was doing wrong. As a second grader, all I wanted to do was please my teacher and make her proud of me.

Every day, my entire class recited the alphabet. Sometimes, we even got to sing. You'd hear Miss White's classroom, and maybe another one at about the same time of day, intoning the same letters: "A, B, C, D, E, F, G..."

And somewhere in the middle of that chorus, maybe a bit too loud, (But what can I tell you? I loved to sing!) you'd hear me: "B, A, D, F, G, C, D..."

For some reason, my teacher took it very personally that I kept forgetting the correct order of the letters. I would get one quarter of the way through the alphabet and then the letters began jumbling up in my mind. To be honest, I was never sure what came next. After class, my teacher would have me read the alphabet and then ask me to close my eyes and try to recite it by memory. Once again, the harder I tried, the worse it got, and the worse it got, the more frustrated my teacher became with me.

I told my mom about this, and she said, "Don't worry, son; it's not where you start, but where you finish." Now, I had no idea what that meant, but if my mom wasn't worried, then neither was I. So, when my teacher got mad, I wouldn't worry because I thought, *"It'll come to me one day, and then all this gobbledygook will make sense."*

One Day, I will pay attention better; One Day, I'll be a better student; and One Day, my teacher will be proud of me. Every day I would go to school with blind faith because... One Day, everything that the teacher wrote on the board and everything she said would magically make sense to me. I just had to hang in there. But what I wasn't aware of was that, as far as my teacher was concerned, I was already finishing last. She was tired of me not getting what she was teaching, and she had a plan.

Instead of having us all recite the alphabet out loud, she called on me to come to the front of the class. I wasn't sure why, but this was the first time she had called on me the entire school year, so I was hoping it was a good sign. When I got to the front of the room, she told me to face the class, so I couldn't see the alphabet on the board. Then she told me to recite the entire alphabet out loud in front of the entire class.

"What? Now!? In front of everybody?"

"Right now, Scotty, and don't make any mistakes."

I swallowed and looked out over the faces of my class-mates. There was Barbara. Smiling. There was Jeffrey, looking bored as ever. There was Anne, playing with her hair.

"A, B, C, D, E... F... G... I, J, K, M, Q... P..." But I'd forgotten what came next. I panicked: "C... ah... could I use the bathroom?"

She looked at me, with fire in her eyes, and said, "No, not until you finish reciting the alphabet correctly."

I might never pee again.

"A, B, D, Q, M... C... B..."

"Again. This time concentrate."

And she repeated that at least four, probably five times. Every time I slipped up, she'd say those words. The fire in her eyes would glow brighter and brighter as I struggled harder and harder.

Then she said the worst thing I had ever heard come out of her mouth: "Just close your eyes and see the letters in your head." Crap. I closed my eyes and I saw gray. I opened my eyes in a panic but was told to close them again. Oh, great. This time when I closed my eyes, I saw a green field with butterflies, a jungle with mysterious creatures, and a waterfall leading up to a tree house where I wished I could have been at that very moment. Well, at least it wasn't a gray jungle, but I also didn't see the stupid alphabet either.

"Scotty, stop right there. This is not the time to be a class clown. I need you to stop horsing around and recite the alphabet."

"But I am..."

24

The entire class burst out laughing. I thought the teacher would make them stop. To my horror, she did not make them stop; she made me stay up in front of everyone while they continued to laugh at me. When I looked at her for help, I realized she was laughing too.

So, this is what hell feels like.

That night at dinner, I told my dad what had happened at school that day. "Son," he said, "you have to try harder. The ABCs aren't that tough. I mean, your brother can say them just fine." And then my younger brother proceeded to dutifully recite the entire alphabet right there at the table.

My appetite disappeared. There was something wrong with me.

"Wait a second, Mr. D; you didn't know you were dyslexic?" asked James.

"Nope. In those days, the late 1950s and early 1960s, everybody was taught the same way. And if you didn't learn like everyone else, you were out of luck and sometimes even held back a grade."

"Were you ever held back, Mr. D?" Grace asked.

5.

SECOND, SECOND GRADE

T he last two years of school hadn't gone very well at all. Nevertheless, I was excited to have all that behind me, and decided that third grade was going to be my year.

Third grade was going to be the year when everything clicked, when everything would at last make sense. In third grade, I was finally going to fit in and become the student I knew I could be—the student my mother knew I could be. No pressure...

(Okay, a lot of pressure.)

Even though I was only eight years old, I wanted so desperately to be accepted. I wanted to be accepted by my classmates and my teachers. I wanted to be recognized as a good student, as a competent student, and most of all... an intelligent student. But when the new school year started, and everyone in my class moved down the hall to the third grade classroom except for me, I knew the jig was up. They had caught me; they'd figured it out. Those kids in preschool were right. I was dumb, and I was stuck

26

doing second grade again. My mom tried hard to convince me that I wasn't dumb. She said that staying back a year didn't make me stupid or even slow, but I didn't believe her; I felt defeated.

I had the same teacher as before, in the same classroom, and the same grade. The only difference was that last year's first-graders were now my classmates, and my former classmates were now third-graders. And boy, they made sure to remind me of it out on the playground during recess.

"Hey dummy, how's second grade... again?"

"Are you learning anything in second grade? Oh, wait a second... you can't learn at all, ha ha!"

After about a week of school, I realized that it was easier to give up than to try. I stopped asking questions and stopped talking in class. I wanted to become invisible, and so I did. Into the Shadows I went. It was safer that way.

During recess, just like in years past, I tried to find places in the yard where no one else was playing. Whenever I was in school, I just wanted to disappear. At home, everything was fine; my mom always treated me like my brothers and sister. I felt important and cared for when I was with my family. Unfortunately, I spent half my life at school, so over the next few years, I had plenty of motivation to put together some very useful self-defense strategies.

Rule Number One: Never talk in class.

Rule Number Two: If you were going to be called on in class, try to get excused for the bathroom.

Rule Number Three: (The most important rule of all!) Be sick as often as possible.

This was the year I first developed and honed my acting skills. I had the ability to fake fevers, stomach pains, and even various bodily injuries. Once my mother became aware of my scams and started sending me off to school, I began performing for an even wider audience. The members of this audience included the classroom teacher, the playground supervisors, the school nurse, the cafeteria workers, the janitor, the principal, my classmates, and anyone else who would listen to me whine and beg for deliverance from my ever-unfolding cornucopia of maladies. I thought that I was fooling everyone with all my lies and exaggerations.

"Where's your homework, Scotty?" my teacher inquired.

"I hurt my wrist last night protecting my dog from a rabid raccoon. I punched it in the face and I sprained my wrist and it hurt so bad that I couldn't write and do my homework."

"What did your parents say?"

"Ummmm... I didn't want to bother them. But the raccoon ran away, and my dog is fine."

"What's wrong this time, Scotty?" asked the school nurse.

"I think I ate something rotten in the cafeteria at lunch today. My stomach feels like a baby dragon is trying to claw its way out of my tummy."

"Maybe I should call your mother to come get you."

"Oh, no... if I just stay in here until my test is over, I'm sure I'll feel better."

"Is anyone in the bathroom?" asked the school janitor.

"Just me," I replied from one of the stalls.

"Let me guess... 'Scotty. Second grade.' It must be test time."

Most of my energy was devoted to getting out of the situation I was in and back into the Shadows where I was comfortable and felt safe. I was continually reminded that I wasn't good enough to move into third grade with all the "normal" kids. But using my three golden rules—don't talk, pee a lot, and always be sick—I was able to make it through second grade this time. I thought it was thanks to the strategies I had developed, but in reality, the school wouldn't hold me back another year and didn't know what to do with me, so they just passed me along.

James confessed, "I used to fake injuries all the time to get out of school."

"I pretended to be sick to get out of my old school, too," added Grace.

"When you went to third grade, did it get any better?" James inquired.

6.

LAST PICKED

In third grade, I wanted to be good at something so badly, and that's exactly what I was: *so bad at everything*... even outside on the playground. I was a triple threat: Couldn't jump, couldn't shoot, and couldn't throw. I still had no idea what to do at recess. I felt like I was too stupid to even understand the simplest of things. I mean, holy cow, who doesn't know what to do at recess? I felt like I was the only one who was clueless. Sounds like something out of a country song: "My baby's too dumb to play at recess, but he's smart enough to play with me."

I can joke about this now, but at the time, it was just another example of how inadequate I felt compared to everyone else. Even while playing tag, I was either too slow or I didn't understand what I was supposed to do.

"Hey Scotty, let's Ro-Sham-Bo to see who's IT," said Johnny.

"Ro-Sham-What?" I asked.

"You know, Rock, Paper, Scissors. The person who loses is IT."

No matter how many times the rules were explained to me, I couldn't quite get a handle on them. So, I was IT... a lot!

One day, the boys in my class decided to start a kickball game. I thought to myself, this game looks easy enough; even I can do this. Just kick the ball and run. The main thing you have to do is summed up right there in the name: kick... ball.

The kids all lined up, so I got in line too, and then they picked the two team captains. Just like all the other kids in line, I worried about how long it would be before I was picked. The important thing to remember when joining a team at recess was that the sooner you were picked, the better a player you were in the eyes of every kid out there. And, of course, the later you got picked, the worse you were in every other player's eyes. Now, I wasn't naïve; I knew I wouldn't get picked first or second. I figured I'd be a good fourth or fifth round pick, but definitely no lower than sixth.

Before I lined up for this recess team, whenever I had watched the other kids pick teams, I'd always felt bad for the last two kids picked. I never imagined in my wildest dreams that I would ever be one of those two kids... and yet suddenly there I was, with just one other player left waiting beside me.

Just when I thought things couldn't get any worse, the two team captains started fighting over me. Which sounds good... except that they weren't fighting about which one would get me, but which one *wouldn't* get me; neither team wanted me and they were trying to make a trade so they wouldn't have to pick me. I was mortified!

And then it happened. One team captain said: "Okay, if I have to take that retard guy, I want your number one pick."

Without any hesitation, the other team captain answered, "Deal."

I turned around and ran as fast as I could. Where I went, I don't remember, but I do know one thing: I never came back, and never joined another pickup game in elementary school again. And the worst part of all was that I was beginning to believe what the kids and teachers were saying about me. I *was* slow, stupid, and retarded. I was the last pick.

"Wow, Mr. D." Frowning, James asked, "How did you not give up? I know I would've."

7.

SCHOOL VERSUS HOME

When I think back on my school days, I wonder how I survived. I lived in two worlds: One world, School, was horrible. I would do anything not to believe the things people said about me there. But the other world, Home, was completely different, and it was because of my mom. My mother believed in me completely. She believed that if I just held on, one day things would make sense and the pieces would fit together. If I just held on long enough, I would belong. I would fit in.

My mother believed this, but I didn't. Mothers are supposed to say nice things about their kids. That's their job.

My mother was a San Francisco Bay Area reporter and a feature writer. Her job was to write stories about people and to make them interesting. She had an amazing gift for writing and communicating feelings to readers. For a petite woman, she was brave, had a huge heart, and passionately showed her love like a mother hawk would for its young. With her present, our nest was protected, and I felt safe. Though she had the fierce dedication of a bird of prey, she never showed any signs of ruthlessness. No matter the circumstances, her calm presence eased any situation.

Mom was exceptionally smart, and had one of the largest vocabularies of anyone I knew. I didn't realize it at the time, but it was my mother's language mastery that led me to take my first step out of the Shadows. Mom used her vocabulary words around me all the time. She never once dumbed down a sentence. If I didn't understand something, she would explain it until I understood the meaning and could use it in everyday conversation.

Thanks to her informal English lessons, between the third and fifth grades the size of my own vocabulary went straight through the roof. Suddenly, I was able to understand what adults were saying. I could understand my mom and dad's dinner discussions, and I could even understand "big words" employed by my classroom teachers.

At this time in school, I discovered that whenever two or more adults wanted to talk about students without leaving the classroom, they would turn to more advanced vocabulary. So instead of saying, "Scott was not able to understand or keep up with the other students during today's lesson. I wonder if this is too hard for him?" they would say, "Scott is demonstrating the inability to comprehend or process the data presented in today's lesson. Maybe this placement is too strenuous for him."

Even though my mother's patient training helped me understand what the teachers were saying to each other, I still couldn't keep up with what they were writing on the chalkboard. "Don't write what you can't spell!" my fourth grade teacher insisted. Well, if those were the rules, then my advanced vocabulary wasn't going to be any help in the classroom. And if I used my "big words" outside at recess to let my classmates know that

"I feel like regurgitating what I just ingested after consuming that putrid lunch," I would be laughed at or pounded into the ground (or both). So even though my mother had given me this great gift, what was the point?

Elementary education in the early 1960s relied heavily on rote memorization. A student was expected to look at a word, or a number, or even a letter, and keeping looking at it repeatedly so that it stuck in their brain. At least, that was the theory. The teacher would tell me, "4 × 4 = 16. Look at it, memorize it. Look at it, memorize it." Then, come the day of the test, I would sit there thinking "4 times 4 equals..." Blank. Nothing. Zilch. I had to somehow magically memorize all this stuff that didn't make any sense to me.

What made all this so frustrating was that in the other world, back at home, I wasn't stupid or dumb. In fact, I was witty, intelligent, creative, funny, and had a wonderful imagination and sense of humor. There weren't just two worlds in which I survived, there also appeared to be two Scotts: the one in elementary school, who felt like a roughly jammed-together puzzle that never fit together as a picture, and the other Scott, at home, where that same puzzle made sense and aspired to be a piece of art. In that world I was confident, achieved what I set out to do, and, most importantly, was happy with myself.

My mom and I loved watching movies together. In third grade, we went to see *The Music Man*. There was nothing quite as impressive to me as the marching band that appeared at the end of that movie. Thanks to the magic of Hollywood, this bunch of misfits and troublemakers turned into a fully formed and coordinated hundred-piece marching band. From that moment on, all I wanted was to be in a marching band. I didn't care what instrument I played; I just wanted to be in one.

I soon tried the trumpet, but my brass teacher said I shouldn't continue with it because I was going to need braces. So, to my family's chagrin, I turned to the drums. By the fourth grade, I was able to play in the school orchestra. I wasn't very good, but I was loud, and I loved it. I couldn't read music very well either, but the more I practiced hitting the drumsticks on the drum—or the phonebook, or the walls, or anything else that was in sight—the better I got.

With the exception of that kickball nightmare back in third grade, I discovered that when I performed and repeated a physical activity, it would stick if I kept doing it. If I stopped practicing for a week, I would lose everything that I had learned, and I would have to start all over again. I began to call this the "Use It or Lose It Syndrome." I did not want to lose my ability to play the drums, so I wouldn't stop practicing. I was determined to reach my goal of being in a marching band.

As a family, my mother encouraged us to put on plays and skits for holiday functions. I loved that too, especially when we could make up our own lines instead of memorizing them. "Alien's First Christmas" was one of my favorites. I played the alien whose spaceship collided with Santa Claus on Christmas Eve, destroying his sleigh. Santa was worried Christmas would be ruined, until I came up with the ingenious idea to use my spaceship to help him deliver all the presents, thereby saving the day.

"You mention your mom a lot, Mr. D. What about your dad?" James asked. "I know you have one; you have a picture of you and him, when you were a little boy, on your desk. You look just like him."

"Well, not only do I look like my dad," I responded, "I also learn like my dad."

"Was he dyslexic too?" Grace asked.

"My dad had a real hard time in school like I did. But in those days, back in the 1930s and 1940s, if you had any academic struggles in school you were guided toward a trade instead of pursuing college. My dad wanted to be a pilot and a writer, but whenever he would take any of the given tests for flight training or for journalism, he would fail. Many of his dreams were blocked by his inability to take tests. According to my aunt, his parents were very disappointed in him and rode him very hard. After flunking out of college for the second time, he left home and wound up in Alaska. At that time, between about 1945 and 1955, Alaska was only a territory of the United States, and had different rules about being a bush pilot and writing for a newspaper. So, in Alaska, he was able to fly and write without having any formal education or degrees."

"It sounds like your dad was able to follow his dreams after all," James said.

"He did, but he hated that part of himself. I think he always felt that he let his parents down and that he was a failure because he wasn't successful in school. My dad was able to work as a reporter and support a family despite his academic failures. But after his first born—that would be me—started having the same problems in school that he did, it brought up all his feelings of inadequacy and self-doubt, and this caused a real rift between the two of us. He was just as hard on me as his parents had been on him. I never seemed to do anything right in his eyes. I think it was because I reminded him of everything that he hated about himself."

Unhappy memories flooded my mind...

"How could you get yourself stuck in your zipper, Scotty?" my dad asked with disapproval as he yanked on the fly of my dress pants. As a six-year-old I had wanted to show my dad how grown-up I was by dressing myself for church, but I had forgotten my underwear. "Are you stupid? Only babies put on their pants without underwear," he added.

I recall a number of occasions when my dad cut me down to size for nothing more than suffering from the same problem he'd wrestled with his entire life.

"Scott!" my dad yelled from underneath the car, "I told you to hand me a wrench, not a screwdriver! Are you dumb or just not paying attention? This is the last time that I'll let you help me."

Even as an adult, he couldn't acknowledge my success.

"Hey, Dad," I said excitedly over the phone, "I'm on the front page of the Sunday newspaper. I was voted one of the Top Five Teachers in the Bay Area." I waited for a response but heard only silence. "Have you seen it?" I asked.

"Yes," my dad responded. "But it's not you on the front page." I was confused. Maybe he had the wrong paper?

"I'm doing a handstand, and there are kids surrounding me, and..."

Dad interjected. "I only see some clown on the front page."

Pushing away these uncomfortable memories, I returned to my conversation with Grace and James.

"Loving someone for who they are is really hard to do," I confessed. "I hated my dad for the longest time, and I blamed him for not giving me the emotional support that I needed while growing up. I just wanted his approval and acceptance, but it seemed like everything I did was never good enough for him.

"One day when I was complaining to my wife for the ump-teenth time about my dad, she finally had enough. She said to me, 'He is who he is. Love him or hate him, but this is who he is. The way he treated you when you were young was terrible, but you know why he did it. If you keep holding on to this, you will never be able to let it go and move past it. You can either continue to use this as an excuse for the rest of your life and stay angry at him, or accept him for who he is and move forward.'

"I took my wife's advice. Even though my dad and I had a strained relationship while I was growing up, it did get better between us. He became a friend and a fantastic grandfather much later in life than I might've liked, but sometimes that's how it is. We even began to bond over being dyslexic."

"That explains why he had struggles in school," said Grace.

Seeming to want to change the subject, James asked, "I know you had struggles too, Mr. D, but wasn't there ever anything that you looked forward to doing at school?"

"Well, there was one thing…" I began, grateful to be moving on.

8.

Turn Left—NO! Your Other Left!

My elementary school had a large student body, and from Monday to Friday students would descend upon the building from every corner of the neighborhood. To make sure they all arrived safely, our school selected a group of volunteer crossing guards. In my eyes, becoming a crossing guard was a huge honor and responsibility. I wanted to belong to something important and do something worthwhile in school, and becoming a crossing guard seemed like the perfect place to start.

To serve as a crossing guard, you had to be in the fifth or sixth grade. In all those years leading up to fifth grade, I watched the uniformed crossing guards march as a six-person unit out to their assigned duties. Marching and a uniform? This was the closest thing I had to being in a marching band, so I was all in. And as a member of the crossing guard, you got to wear a yellow hat, red sweater, white sash, and sometimes even carry a giant stop sign. To an eleven-year-old student desperately in search of approval, this job had everything going for it.

I couldn't wait until fifth grade when I could finally join. That magical day came at last when this gigantic and very official-looking policeman came to our school. All the kids who wanted to volunteer for crossing guard duty were asked to come out onto the basketball courts after school.

Towering over us, the policeman said in a booming voice, "It is a great honor to be a member of the crossing guard." *You've got that right,* I thought. "You get to wear a uniform." *(Cool!)* "March in parades." *(Oh my, it couldn't get any better than this!)* "And you get to get out of school early." **(Sold.)** I finally found something that I was made to do: I was going to be the best dang crossing guard there ever was.

I put all my hopes and dreams of ever fitting in into serving in the crossing guard. Given my history, you would probably conclude that this didn't sound realistic, but I felt I had to do it. This made what the officer said next even more devastating.

"There is only one thing you have to do for me." I waited, holding my breath. "Know your left foot from your right." And then he laughed out loud and all the other kids started laughing too.

"That's easy," one kid said, "because everybody knows their left from their right."

Oh no... no, no, no. Not that—anything but that. My dream of being a crossing guard was over before it began.

Right face. Left face. Two simple commands, but when the pressure was on and people were watching me, I just couldn't do it. It was like I was being asked to do calculus—it just wasn't going to happen. When standing in a corner by myself I could figure it out. I could turn left; I could turn right. But marching down the street with the pressure of trying not to screw up was just as hard as seeing all those letters and numbers in my head: everything jumbled up and went gray.

The officer had us practice in three lines. He stood in front of us with his hands behind his back, the sunlight reflecting off his badge. Then, with a booming voice, he commanded, "Left face!" In unison, thirty kids turned left with beautiful precision and coordination, moving as one group. There was just one exception: me. After we all came to a stop, I was standing face to face, nose to nose with the person behind me. What, how did this happen? Utter silence fell upon the blacktop and lingered there like a stalking tiger, eager to find and pounce on me.

I didn't know what to do. Should I turn around and ruin this perfectly coordinated formation, or should I just stay there, face-to-face with this kid I didn't know, and hope nobody would notice? I decided to go with Door Number Two: stay where I was and not move a muscle. I was just one of thirty kids and was in the back of the line where I was sure our commanding officer wouldn't even notice me. Suddenly, a voice thundered like a volcano. That's when I realized that Door Number One might have been a better choice. The voice started low, but then exploded in sound. "Hey you! Stupid! I said left, not right."

I didn't move. I hoped, prayed even, that maybe there was another kid who had also turned the wrong way and that the officer was referring to him. Maybe if I slowly turned around he wouldn't notice me. Before I could put this plan into motion, the sunlight was blotted out by a giant shadow, as if the day had turned to night. I looked up to see the flaring nostrils of the officer looking down on me.

"Are you deaf, too? I'm talking to you!" The jig was up, so I turned slowly to face in the other direction. But that wasn't good enough for the officer. With that booming voice of his, he demanded explanations I couldn't possibly give. "What's wrong with you? Don't you know your left from your right?" Looking up at him, I gave him my most sincere smile and shrugged my shoulders.

He wasn't pleased. "You have to be in the fifth grade to be a crossing guard, not the second. Come back when you grow up." All the kids laughed. Why did he have to say second grade, of all the grades? He could have picked any other grade, why second?

I can't remember exactly what happened in the minutes that followed; it was all a haze and a blur. I do remember being at home crying on my mother's shoulder. I told her the whole story, how everything went blank and I couldn't remember how to tell my left from my right. I told my mom I was not going back to school ever again and my dream of being a crossing guard was over. Who was I fooling? The officer was right. I was too stupid to be a crossing guard. I couldn't even figure out my left from my right.

That night, after dinner, my mom got everybody together and we started playing one of our favorite family games: Spoons. This game was sort of like Musical Chairs, but with playing cards and spoons instead of music and chairs. The person left without a spoon at the end lost the round.

Everybody was given four cards to start out. The object of the game was to get four matching cards. The player with the deck of cards would pick one up, look at it, and pass it to the next player. Everyone would keep passing the cards along until someone got four of a kind. Whenever this happened, that person would take one spoon from the pile in the center of the table. Once the first spoon was taken, it was a free for all and whoever was left without a spoon was the loser. It was one of our favorite games to play as a family and we always had lots of fun. But I was surprised to get to play it this evening, since we never played games on a school night.

When the game was over and everybody was going off to bed, Mom pulled me aside and asked, "Scott, have you ever wondered why I have never lost at Spoons?" It was true; my mother never ever lost at Spoons. Come to think of it, she never got four of a kind either, but somehow she always got a spoon.

She could tell by the confused look on my face that I had no idea how she had mastered this feat. With a devilish grin, she said, "I have a strategy."

"You have a strategy? Why? I thought the point of the game was not to think but just go for it."

"The truth is, Scott, it's hard for me to do two things at once. Watching my cards as well as keeping an eye on the spoons is a real challenge for me. Do you get what I mean?"

"Not really," I confessed.

My mother looked around to see if anyone else could hear her besides me. Lowering her voice, she whispered, "I have a secret. I don't ever look at my cards."

"What?" I asked, shocked. "Isn't that cheating?"

"The object of the game is to have a spoon at the end of the round, right? Well, I don't ever look at my cards; instead I watch the spoons, and as soon as the first one is taken, I reach for the next one. The object to me is to *win*. I am not the biggest or the fastest or even the smartest in this family, so I had to come up with a plan to outsmart you guys."

"Really?"

My mom looked me straight in the eyes. "Have I ever lost?" Then she asked me, "Do you know why we played tonight?"

I told her that I did think it was strange playing on a school night. Then my mom said something that I didn't think was possible for a woman who didn't enjoy or understand sports. She said, "Son, life is like a football game. If you don't have a plan, you're going to get the crap knocked out of you."

I sat there with my mouth wide open. I didn't know what to think or what to say. I'd just found out two things about my mother that I hadn't known before: she liked to win, and she knew what football was. My world had just turned upside down.

Mom offered me a smile. "Let's take a walk."

We had been walking around the neighborhood for about ten minutes when she asked, "Do you still want to be a crossing guard?" I reminded her I wanted to be a crossing guard more than anything in the world, but that I was not smart enough to be one because the officer said that I was too stupid. She stopped and looked at me like I had just hit her in the face with a baseball bat.

"Never say that again."

"Say what again?" I asked.

"That you're stupid," she repeated, more firmly. I'd never seen her this angry before. "Never ever say you're stupid or dumb or lazy again, because you are not."

There were tears in her eyes, but I wasn't sure why. I didn't know what I had said wrong. My mom put her hands on my shoulders, not breaking eye contact, and said, "You are not stupid, and you can do anything that you want to; you just have to come up with the right plan." She took a breath. "Scott, every problem has a solution. Just like in Spoons, I had a strategy, a plan for winning. You want to be a crossing guard, you have to come up with a plan for remembering your lefts and rights while under pressure."

45

Then it hit me. We were playing Spoons that night because she wanted to show me that if you have a plan, you can solve anything. So, for the first time in my life, I started thinking about how I could solve a problem—this problem. And I got an idea.

When I went back to practice the next day, I was worried that the officer would kick me out on sight, but he didn't seem to notice my presence. When he told us to line up, I got right behind one of my friends who knew his left from his right. I did not listen for the commands; I just watched my friend's feet. When he took a step forward, I took a step forward with the same foot. When he turned, I turned in the same direction. Every time he stepped, I stepped. Every time he turned, I turned. He marched, I marched. Whichever foot he put out first, I put out first. I mimicked everything he did. We marched around the blacktop, turning left, turning right, all over the playground. I didn't miss a turn; I was like everyone else.

At the end of our marching, the officer walked back and forth, with his hands behind his back, looking at all of us. When he got to me, he stopped. I thought it was all over. Instead, he said, "Nice job, fifth grader." Then he moved on. And that was it.

For the next two years, I was a member of the crossing guard. I continued to watch and model myself after the moves of the other members. It wasn't easy, and I made a lot of mistakes, but I learned one thing: *Never give up.* Oh, and also that Mom was right. For every problem there was a solution, if you figure out the right plan. I never thought I could learn until that day. But now, learning meant coming up with the right strategy. For the first time in my academic life, I'd figured something out.

"We're learning about strategies too, in Miss Jones' class," said James.

"Since you learned how to solve problems by using strategies, I guess the rest of elementary school must've gone smoothly for you, right?" Grace asked.

"That would have been nice, but there were more obstacles to come."

9.

THE SPELLING BEE

Sixth grade was finally here, and I was thrilled to have the end of elementary school in sight. If I could just get to junior high school, I was sure things would be different. With the exception of second grade, so far I had slipped through the cracks. I was a quiet, well-behaved kid who was functioning well below grade level. My teachers knew I was struggling, but they either didn't care or didn't know how to reach me. My parents were aware I was behind, and did all they could to support me. They helped me with my homework and sent me to a tutor. But none of this made any difference. After all, it was the 1960s. No teacher was trained to deal with kids like me.

To my horror, my sixth-grade teacher was the same one I had in fourth grade, Mrs. Career. As soon as I entered the classroom on that first day, I knew she remembered me, too. "Have we learned to focus yet, Scotty?" she asked. "Are you going to pay attention this year, or are you just going to look out the window like you did all of fourth grade?" She didn't wait for me to answer. Instead, she smiled. "No, no... not this year. This year I'm expecting big things from you."

Wow. No pressure there, I thought. And don't call me Scotty. As far as I was concerned, my name was Scott. I was a sixth grader and a member of the crossing guard. Teacher or not, that wasn't any way to talk to another valuable member of the academic community. I was determined not to let her get to me this year, not during my last year here. I'd survive all this just fine.

Seeing Mrs. Career back behind the front desk brought back memories about fourth grade that I'd stuffed down deep inside. I recalled that weekly public humiliation, the "Spelling Bee." I hoped she wouldn't bring that back. I had convinced myself that there would not be a Spelling Bee in sixth grade. I had just started noticing girls and, like all sixth-grade adolescent boys, I was desperate to impress them. The last thing I wanted was to do anything embarrassing in front of the class.

By the time sixth grade rolled around, I had gotten good at getting out of embarrassing situations. If I had to read aloud, I either had to go to the bathroom or to the school nurse or to any place that wasn't in the classroom. I kept all my work hidden so no one could see how poorly I performed. Anytime I got an assignment back that was corrected and had a score on it, I made sure no one else could see it. I had developed and honed many survival skills during this time.

The most important thing was not to let anyone know how dumb I was, because by this time, despite my best efforts and my mother's continuing insistence to the contrary, I did believe that I was dumb. The only thing that I truly cared about at school was managing to avoid embarrassment and keep from making a fool of myself in front of my peers. It was critical to my survival that I not be exposed for who I really was: the dunce of the class, always too slow to keep up. I figured if I could just get through the sixth grade without any major embarrassments, I could hide when I got to junior high school.

The junior high school in my town was very big. Six elementary schools fed into one middle school, so I figured it wouldn't be too hard to disappear into the Shadows. I thought that if I could get through the sixth grade unscathed, my secret would be safe.

But it'd be a tough secret to keep, as Mrs. Career was determined to bring back the Spelling Bee for me and my classmates. Crap.

But I could figure this out, right? I was older and wiser now, if not exactly smarter (despite what Mom would have me believe). I had all my strategies in place, and Mrs. Career wasn't going to humiliate me—not this year, not again. However, Mrs. Career had other plans: She'd decided I'd make it through at least one round of the weekly torture.

I guess she'd taken it very personally that in fourth grade I'd never gotten past the first round. So, one Monday morning when we were just arriving at school, Mrs. Career came up to me and whispered in my ear, "This year, Scotty, you're going to make it past the first round in my Spelling Bee."

For our first Spelling Bee of the year, Mrs. Career lined us all up against the wall, just like she had in fourth grade. One by one, the victims trudged up to the front of the class to receive their word. I was really starting to get nervous because, through-out my illustrious career in Spelling Bees, I'd never managed to spell one word correctly.

It was almost my turn; two classmates ahead of me, Katie, the stunning blonde, stepped into position. Mrs. Career, sitting in the front row (which seemed odd, as I was accustomed to seeing her behind a large desk with her back to the blackboard), said, "Katie, your word is 'caliphate.'"

"*What!?*" I thought. What's a caliphate? Is that some kind of elephant, or perhaps the fate of people living in Earthquake-prone California? But Katie just smiled. If she'd stood any straighter, you'd have mistaken her for a statue of Barbie.

"Caliphate. C... A... L..." I can't recall all the letters she proceeded to deliver with the precision of an Olympic diver. I remember thinking, "*Get it wrong! Get it wrong! Just get it wrong.*" "...E. Caliphate."

"Very good, Katie!" Mrs. Career smiled the smile of one who'd anticipated the outcome. There would be no surprises today. Except for... me.

When it was my turn, I slowly walked up to the front of the class. I felt like I was walking to my doom, but Mrs. Career was smiling at me and I had no idea why. I kept remembering what she had said: "This year, Scotty, you're going to make it past the first round." What did she have in store for me?

So there I was, standing in front of my entire class with all eyes on me. I felt like I was in front of a firing squad, and I could hear my heart beating in my ears. Maybe I was having a heart attack. At least having a heart attack would get me out of this Spelling Bee. But to my dismay, my heart held out. Mrs. Career looked at me with a big smile on her face and said, "Scotty, your word to spell is 'does.'"

Time stood still. Did she just say "does?" *I know that word, I can spell "does!"* I was saved. For the first time, I knew I would make it past the first round. Life was good, and I was not going to be embarrassed.

I stood up in front my classmates, facing them with confidence. With pride and dignity, I opened my mouth wide and spelled my word, loud and proud: "D... O... S... E, does."

Katie gasped, while Johnny and Chris giggled. Perhaps they were as thrilled as I was. I did it. I made it. I didn't have to take that long walk of shame back to my desk. For the first time ever, I could get back in line with all the second-round kids. I looked at my teacher for her approval, but I was shocked to see the expression on her face. She was no longer smiling. In fact, she looked like I had just slapped her in the face or kicked her dog, or possibly both. What did I do wrong? I spelled the word correctly, didn't I? You could hear a pin drop; it was like everyone was holding their breath, all their eyes on me.

After what felt like an eternity, my teacher spoke in a controlled but furious voice. "Spell 'does' again Scotty, and this time spell it right!" snarled Mrs. Career.

"I—I did spell it right."

"Spell it. Again."

I slowly spelled it again: "D... O... S... E, does." I looked at my teacher again. Her face was still contorted into a scowl and now it looked as though all the blood had drained out of it.

She slowly said to me, "Write it on the board."

"Ummm... okay," I said, nervously turning to face the chalkboard. I picked up a small piece of white chalk and in minute letters wrote the word: d o s e. I put the chalk down and reluctantly faced my teacher.

Now, I had heard the idiom "blowing your top," but I had never actually *seen* anyone blow their top. Believe me, it is not a pretty sight.

At first, my teacher couldn't talk; she just started making hissing and gurgling sounds. With her eyes bugging out of her head, she finally managed to snarl, "Get out of my classroom!" I was shocked.

"I'm confused, Mrs. Career. Where would you like me to go?"

"To the Principal's Office, you moron, and don't come back."

In all my years in elementary school, I had never been sent to the principal's office. But the look on Mrs. Career's face told me I had better get going, so I put my head down and walked out of class while all the kids laughed and pointed at me. I still had no idea why she had sent me out of the class. Word must have traveled quickly, because when I got to the principal's office, her secretary told me to sit down and wait for my mother to come.

"Why is my mother coming to school?" I asked the secretary.

"Because you are being suspended from school for disrespectful behavior."

"Suspended?"

My whole world started spinning. I remember feeling like Dorothy in *The Wizard of Oz* when the tornado lifted her house and spun it in circles. But my teacher wasn't swirling outside while riding a bicycle with the dust and the cows. Instead, she stood at the center of the funnel. Far away as she was, I could see her—feel her glaring at me like I'd done something to wrong her personally. Guess I wasn't in Kansas anymore. And, as it turned out, I wasn't going to be in school for a while, either.

After my mom picked me up from school, she took me out for lunch. I still couldn't figure out what had just happened. I asked my mom if she knew why I'd been suspended from school and what I had done wrong. My mother told me that my teacher thought I was intentionally being disrespectful and that I was showing her up in front of the class by deliberately misspelling "does."

"What? I thought I was spelling 'does' correctly, and why would I try to embarrass Mrs. Career? The last thing I wanted to do was to piss off my teacher. Mom, none of this day has made any sense to me."

Apparently my suspension was only for twenty-four hours, because the next day when I returned to school I was sent to see a special teacher to take special tests. I went to a different classroom on the school campus where this teacher administered a variety of tests which included reading and writing comprehension, fill in the blank, multiple choice, and something called the Rorschach test, to name a few. My school was finally trying to figure out where I belonged and what to do with me. Mom said that I had to take these tests because I was special. I was beginning to think that "special" was code for "He's different, and we don't know what to do about it."

I was relieved when I finished all the testing, but was fraught with anticipation while waiting for the results. What would these test results show? What would happen to me? When the test results finally came in, they showed I was below grade level on all my subjects. I was at about a second-grade level, straight across the board.

The teachers came up with a plan. I would be reviewing material that would be at my academic level but stay in the same grade. I finally got to go back to the classroom. But to my embarrassment, I didn't go back to my classroom; I went to the other sixth-grade classroom with a new teacher and new classmates.

"Class, let's welcome Scott," said Mrs. Snow. "He's coming from Room 6 and he will be spending the rest of the year with us." She then escorted me to the back of the room where I had my own chair and desk separate from the rest of the kids. Mrs.

Snow seemed very nice, but I felt like I was still in trouble, and that moving classes was part of the punishment.

On the first day in my new class, Mrs. Snow told the kids to take out their reading books. Each kid opened their desk tops, pulled out a book, and began reading to themselves. Silent reading, good; I could do that—pretend to read. I wasn't going to be embarrassed after all.

While sitting at my desk waiting for the teacher to bring me my book, my mind started to wander. I looked around at the other students. The girl closest to me was reading *Moby Dick*. Cool, I thought; a giant whale attacking innocent people and chewing them into bits. Sounds like fun to me. I wondered what book I would get.

As all the other kids continued to read quietly, Mrs. Snow came over to me, leaned in, and whispered in my ear: "I hope this book won't be too hard for you." She placed the book on my desk and left. I looked at the book with horror. Opening it and reluctantly flipping through the pages, I realized this was *See Spot Run*, the book we read in second grade.

Even though I still had trouble reading, I figured my new teacher must have made a mistake and given me the wrong book, so I raised my hand politely. When she called on me, I stood up and said, "I think you gave me the wrong book to read."

She looked at me, as well as every other kid in the room, and spoke clearly for all to hear: "No, Scott, there's no mistake; that is the book you're supposed to read."

The girl sitting closest to me, the one who was reading *Moby Dick*, leaned over and looked at my book. "Hey, you guys," she said loud enough so the entire class could hear, "Scotty's reading *See Spot Run*. That's a second grade book!" With that, everyone laughed.

And there it was: Within the first couple weeks of sixth grade, I had learned a very important lesson. I was Special. Special used to mean something good, but now it meant that I was different and not as good as the other kids. I spent the rest of that year in the back of the classroom feeling humiliated and doing the same work that I had struggled through in second grade. All the other kids were doing sixth-grade work and preparing for junior high school while I was still doing second-grade work, preparing for... nothing. I no longer looked forward to junior high, and I sure as heck did not want to be Special.

"Wow, Mr. D, I had no idea how hard it was for you," said James.

"Well, before I got here, I was held back two grades!" Grace seemed almost pleased. "I was and still am the oldest in my class. And I don't think all that much has changed since you were in school. The kids at my old school used to call me 'Ed,' short for special ed, and the teachers didn't do anything about it. I don't want to be special anymore, just normal. I hate when kids in my neighborhood judge me for being different. I just want to fit in."

"I know how you guys feel. To this day I still reverse letters when I spell... isn't that Special!"

"I reverse letters too, Mr. D," said James.

"My problem is with numbers," added Grace. "I reverse them all the time and it's really embarrassing, especially when I'm at the store trying to buy something. I look like such an idiot."

"So, Mr. D, how did you fit in?" James asked.

"I hate to admit this, but..."

10.

"THEY"

Survival was the most important thing to me, and so far I was not doing such a great job of it. No matter where I went at school—the classroom, playground, or cafeteria—I felt like I didn't fit in. I started getting the feeling *they* were just tolerating my presence. At recess, *they* had to play with me. At lunch, *they* had to sit with me. And in the classroom, *they* had to ignore how "slow" I was and pretend that I was normal just like them.

Who were *they*? They were all the normal kids, all the people that could do things easily and naturally without working hard at it. And truth be told, I wanted to be one of them so badly. I just wanted to be good at something and to have a natural talent. To me, it appeared that everyone else had something they were born to do, and I had nothing. I was naturally good at nothing; I was born to do nothing. This was my perception, not reality. But as far as I was concerned, my perception of myself *was* reality, no matter what my family might say.

And then something changed.

The day started out just like any other day as I performed my usual morning traffic duty with my six-person crossing guard squad. But on this morning, for the first time ever, I got to use one of the large metal STOP signs to control traffic at a very busy intersection. These STOP signs, affixed to long wooden poles, were carried like rifles on the crossing guards' shoulders. When we were told to stop traffic, we stepped out into the street and raised our sign out to the side like a shield. I thought this was one of the coolest things I could do. I had the power to stop traffic, I was in charge, and I had control over something. I wasn't that stupid kid in the back of the room; I was a member of a team. I had a purpose.

On this particular day while I was on duty with my squad, our sergeant blew the whistle, alerting me to go out into the street and hold up my sign. A car was approaching, but instead of slowing down the driver just swerved sharply, knocking my sign out of my hand. Without skipping a beat, the vehicle sped off.

Now, if my memory serves me correctly, this car probably didn't touch me—just my sign—but I didn't expect it to pass so close or, for that matter, to keep moving. My sign flew into the air and I dramatically hit the ground. The street fell silent and everybody looked at me. They weren't laughing at me. They weren't calling me names. They ran up to me to see if I was okay.

"Oh my God, are you hurt?" asked Caroline.

"Can you move? Did you break anything?" asked John.

"Can you walk, or should we carry you?" asked Marvin.

And, like magic, I was one of them—just a normal kid who was hurt. I did scratch my elbow and knee, but these were very minor injuries. Instinctively, I realized I was getting positive attention for being hurt. So, with a captive audience and a knack for the dramatic, I started exaggerating my injuries. The more I exaggerated, the more positive attention I received. At least, that was my perception at the time. Marlon Brando would have been proud.

My squad had to carry me back to school because I was too "crippled" to walk. When my squad carried me to the nurse's office, they had to pass through the crowd of kids attending recess. All the kids on the playground saw me carried, battered and bruised like a war hero. When I was in the nurse's office, lots of people came by to see if I was okay; even the principal checked in on me. This was the same person who had suspended me from school for spelling 'does' wrong. Holy smokes... I was onto something.

For the first time at school, people weren't just putting up with me. I felt like I was a hero because I got hit by a car while doing my duty for the school.

What I learned that day was that I *did* have a skill and a talent, and it served me well: I had a flair for the dramatic. If people knew what had really been going on, some of them might have concluded that I was a liar or a fake; in my head, though, I was just surviving... and anyway, nobody had to know the truth. I did get hit by a car—or at least, my sign did. Was it as bad as I made it out to be? No. But I milked it for all I could, and for the rest of the school year I wasn't "that dummy" or "that retard;" I was "that kid who got hit by a car." And I thought that was really cool.

"Oh my God Mr. D... I can't believe you did that!" exclaimed Grace.

"Did any of your friends ever figure out that you faked it, or were you that good of an actor?" asked James.

"Oh, I thought I was. And it worked at first, but I started to rely on lying to get out of uncomfortable situations. The more I lied, the more people started not believing me."

James was genuinely confused. "When you went to junior high, did you get in trouble for using your imagination?"

"You mean for lying?" Grace corrected him.

11.

JUNIOR HIGH, THANK GOD

No, for me junior high was going to be an escape. An escape from elementary school. An escape from being that dummy in the back of the class. An escape from being that strange kid, the one that didn't fit in and didn't belong. I was psyched. I was pretty sure that I wouldn't see any of the kids from my elementary school again, and I was going to get a bunch of new teachers, not just one for the entire day. So even if the first teacher was bad, I would still have six more chances to get a good one.

Mom told me that Martin Luther King Junior High, in Berkeley, was almost like High School, and that I would have seven periods a day with seven different subjects. I was excited because I was sure that I could find at least two or three subjects I was going to be good in. There just had to be a place where I belonged, and there had to be a subject that I would be good in—there just had to be.

During the first week of school, we all had to take a bunch of placement tests to figure out what level we were in for each subject. *Cool,* I thought. I had a clean slate, and I would get to start all over. One of these tests was an IQ test. That didn't sound too good to me, because I knew what IQ meant, and I also knew that I was about as smart as a sack of hammers.

So it came as a great shock to me and the administration when I scored very high on the IQ test. In fact, they made me retake the placement tests because my IQ score was so much higher than my academic subject levels. What did that mean? I had close to a genius IQ, but academically I placed into second grade. Smart but dumb, wow… only I could manage both at the same time.

I was encouraged, though, because having a high IQ meant I must be smart at something, and with that information surely my new school would put me in classes where I could start actually learning stuff. I would show those teachers in elementary school what they had missed out on. I would be an academic superstar. Watch out world, here I come! *"It's HAMMER time."*

There was only one problem with my theory: the people in charge of assigning classes couldn't figure out why I had scored so high on the IQ test while scoring so low in *all* my academic subjects. It wasn't until years later that researchers would identify high IQ as a component of dyslexia. At the time, my teachers just thought it was a fluke; just another ill-fitting puzzle piece.

When the class list was handed out, all my academic classes for the first semester were taught under a program called Track 4. I didn't know what Track 4 was, but it didn't matter because besides my classes in English, History, and Math, I also got to take Band, Art, and PE. Band class meant I was one step closer to being in the marching band, which was one of my only reasons for wanting to be in school in the first place. Art and PE sounded like fun, too. I didn't know what the letters "PE" stood for, but I did know it had something to do with sports. I loved sports, and despite my lack of success and my totally uncoordinated body, I believed that with a little guidance I would be good at them, possibly great even.

Junior high was going to be fantastic. A new school, new teachers, new classmates, and a new attitude: mine. No more being told that I was stupid, no more being picked last; it was a brand-new year, and I couldn't wait for it to start.

But almost immediately, I noticed something was different about junior high. They separated all the academic subjects into four parts. Track 1 was for kids who had scored high on the tests and were expected to do well in high school and beyond. Track 2 was for those students who needed a little more help but were also expected to do well. Track 3 was for the kids who scored poorly on the placement tests but were *still* expected to do well. And then there was Track 4. According to one of the kids in school, Track 4 was "the dumping ground." It was where you went if they couldn't figure out what to do with you—*The Island of Misfit Toys.*

Every Christmas, my family watched *Rudolph the Red-Nosed Reindeer.* It was my favorite Christmas special on TV. If you've seen it, you might recall that Rudolph is sent to the Island of Misfit Toys because he had a glowing bright red nose, making him different from all the other reindeer. The toys on this island were either broken, didn't work right, or didn't look right. Toys were also sent there for another reason, a painful one: nobody wanted them. Is that what Track 4 was? The Island of Misfit Toys?

When my mom found out I was in all Track 4 academic classes, she went to the principal and school board and insisted that I be retested in all my academic subjects. Now, I might not have said this before, but I suck at taking tests. Nowadays people call it test anxiety. I would crash and burn. And with every test I took, the teacher said, "Don't worry, but I am going to have to time this test." What!? There was a *time limit*? I truly didn't understand why she had to time it. *"Just give me the damn test and let me try to get through it."*

As soon as that clock started, everything went haywire. And just like always, the harder I tried the worse it would get. So despite my high IQ, I tested very poorly in all academic areas.

Take math, for instance; those darn numbers kept jumping around all over the page.

1. 95 × 5 = ___
What I thought:
"I can do this. 59 × 5 = 259"

When it came to English, sometime the letters had a mind of their own.

1. I before E except after C. True or False?
What I saw:
Iebf orE excpe ttafte rCtreuoerfalse?

I tested low in history because my reading comprehension issues prevented me from understanding the questions as quickly as most students. After I finally figured out what each question was asking, it was time to try and write down my answers. Even when I knew the right answers, I couldn't spell the words, and because I couldn't spell the words, my responses would consequently get marked wrong.

For example:

1. During the Revolutionary War, who were the British fighting and why?

What I thought, after puzzling out the question:

"Oh, I know this one; this is easy."

What I wrote:

The colunees of the Amaricas fauth the Britesh to wun there independans form Englund.

Frequently, after taking these gruesome tests, I found myself sitting alone in the cafeteria. My head was spinning, and I felt like running away and hiding. Why was this happening to me again, and what was I doing wrong? I couldn't figure it out. The cafeteria was practically empty. A tall, muscular African American boy with intense brown eyes and a smile that went from ear to ear suddenly sat down at my table. He could have sat anywhere, but he chose to sit right across from me.

"Hey man, how's it going?" he asked.

I was shocked. Most people at school didn't start conversations with me. He looked like one of the cool kids. What could he possibly want with me? Maybe he sat down across from me so he could pick on me.

I panicked.

"Cool," I said, "you?" Boy, was I a great conversationalist.

I figured this kid would get up and leave after my remark, but instead he looked me in the eye and said, "They can't figure out what to do with me either."

I didn't know what he meant, but I didn't want to say anything. I didn't want him to think that I was weird. After what felt like a minute of silence he said, "You don't like taking tests, do you?"

I wanted to sound cool and intelligent, but I was in a total panic. This cool kid wanted to talk to me and I had to make a good first impression, but there was that clock in my head ticking away again: *tick, tock, tick, tock.* This was just like taking a test. So, without thinking, I blurted out the first thing that came to my mind at the top of my lungs.

"F– NO, I don't like taking tests!"

He laughed and said, "You're the first white kid I've talked to. Do all white kids swear so much?"

Then I realized that he thought I was nervous because of his skin color. The truth was I was just afraid that he thought I was stupid.

"My name's Mike. What's yours?"

For the next ten minutes, Mike and I talked. It turns out the administration had made him retake the placement tests because he came from a family where no one had gone to college, and most hadn't gotten out of high school. Even though his test scores were high, they weren't sure if he was going to be college material because of his family history.

That was the first time I realized that I didn't have it so bad and that there were other people out there who were also struggling with problems. I wasn't the only misfit in school. We became friends and hung out as much as we could. After all the test results came in, Mike got into mostly all Track 1 classes and I didn't. But he and I still had something in common: we were both judged by others on the basis of things over which we had no control. I was not alone.

Math, Track 4. English, Track 4. History... wait for it... Track 4. All my academic subjects were still in the lowest level possible.

My first period of the day was English, and I was nervous since I had already missed a few days of class because of the retesting. When I entered my new classroom, there was nobody there, not even a teacher. I looked at the clock. I was on time, wasn't I? In fact, the tardy bell was about to ring. Was I in the wrong room? Was this the right day? And then the bell rang, the door opened, and in flew a bunch of kids—my new classmates.

They were laughing and talking. One kid held a radio playing music. The kids didn't sit down at their desks. Instead, they just started hanging out. Some kids were dancing to the music, some were playing cards, and others were just talking. Looking around, I noticed two things: there wasn't a teacher in the classroom, and I appeared to be the only wimpy kid there. In fact, some of the guys looked tough, and I stuck out like a sore thumb because the last words anyone would use to describe me were "tough" or "street smart." Was I going to live to the end of the period? Then I remembered what I had heard: Track 4 was a dumping ground. So... maybe I was in the right place after all.

I was trying to figure out what to do when the door opened again, and the teacher walked in. Oh, snap; the crap was going to hit the fan now. Instead of getting mad and demanding that the students take their seats, though, the teacher just walked to his desk, sat down, and started reading the paper. To my surprise, our teacher didn't seem to care that the kids in his class weren't paying any attention to him. In fact, I don't think he minded at all.

So, there it was: welcome to Track 4, Scott. Welcome to the world of no expectations. Back into the Shadows I go, back into the Shadows where no one will notice me. I guess it beats a Spelling Bee. But I wasn't sure yet if it was worse to have something expected of me and not be able to do it, or to not be expected to do anything at all.

At first it really bothered me. I was there to learn, after all. My mother kept telling me how smart and gifted I was, and I scored high on my IQ test, so I knew I could learn. The question was, *how* could I learn? That turned out to be a really hard question to answer. My whole elementary academic career consisted of me beating my head against a wall. "See the word in your head!" the teacher would say. Or, "We went over this last week; don't tell me you've already forgotten it?" Okay, I won't tell you. I mean, I was doing the best I could, and it didn't seem to make any difference. I kept hearing, "You're dumb, you're stupid," followed by, "You're not applying yourself. You're not really trying. Maybe you're lazy."

But lazy was the last thing I thought I was, because I tried my best at all times. I'd hoped that when I got to junior high things would be different. Teachers would know how I learned, and they would teach me that way. But it turned out that was just another miscalculation on my part. Not only did they not try to find out how I learned, but it was becoming pretty clear that they didn't even pretend to care.

In Track 4, nobody asked me any questions. Nobody asked me to remember anything, or recite anything, or memorize anything. After a while I got used to that. In fact, I started to like it. No expectations meant I didn't disappoint or embarrass myself. My stomach didn't hurt anymore when I went to school, I didn't have to fake being sick to stay home from school, and I had friends in my classes. In Track 4, we were all in the same boat. Nobody laughed at me if I couldn't spell a word or read a paragraph. I wasn't an outcast or "that strange kid." I was just one of "those" kids, and I belonged. I was no longer beaten up or chased around or even teased.

Track 4 had other advantages. My classmates were the tough kids in school, the ones the other kids stayed away from when they walked down the halls. I soon discovered that when walking with my Track 4 classmates, kids got out of my way, too. Those kids who had harassed and tortured me in elementary school were now the ones who were afraid. Now, I knew they weren't afraid of *me*, but they were definitely afraid of the kids I was *with*. Cool. Forget them! I didn't care; I had finally found a place where I was accepted. That was good enough for me.

So, for the next two years, I went to school and attended class and didn't learn a thing. Nobody expected me to study English, math, history, or science. If I showed up and didn't cause trouble, I passed. And that's exactly what I did. If my school didn't think I was smart or worth the effort to teach, then I wasn't going to put in the effort to learn either, since it obviously didn't matter. I didn't want any help. I didn't want any sympathy. I didn't feel that anyone cared. So, if no one else cared, why should I? It didn't matter anyway. All those teachers and kids in elementary school were right. Anyhow, it was a lot easier being stupid than trying to be smart. Who was I fooling anyway?

My mom was the only one who still believed in me. This was the first time I started really doubting her. After all this time, maybe she was wrong and everybody else was right.

Not being driven by anyone who expected me to do my best, or better than I thought I could do, made school much easier and stress-free. I could just fly through the school days and nobody would notice me. I knew where I stood, I knew who I was, and more importantly, I knew who I wasn't. I wasn't smart, despite my high IQ, I wasn't going to college, and I wasn't going to make a difference with my life. I wasn't going to be noticed in school, and I was fine with that. Even more than before, now school was all about survival—not learning and growing academically—just about getting through.

Grace lowered her voice so only I could hear. "I wish I could go unnoticed, be invisible." She paused to make sure James wasn't listening in on what she was saying. "You were lucky school gave up on you. I know that when I get to high school everyone will notice me, I hate the idea of..."

"What?" James interrupted. "What are you saying, Grace? Why are you whispering?"

Looking shocked and exposed, Grace quickly changed the subject. "Nothing. I wasn't saying anything, you weirdo. Mr. D, I get why you had self-doubt in the classroom, but you're our PE teacher now, so you must have been good at PE, right?"

12

DUDE!
YOU CAN FLUNK PE?

How could anyone flunk physical education? Isn't PE one of those classes that anyone could pass, even a dummy like me? There was only one thing that I thought I could do well: I don't know where I got this feeling from, but I thought I would be good at sports.

By the time I was thirteen years old, I was six feet tall, had size twelve feet, and weighed about 125 pounds. A stiff wind could have blown me over, though, and I had the coordination of a dead gnat. So where I may have gotten this delusional idea that I would naturally be good at sports from, I have no idea. But I had to be good at *something*, and I was sure that something was athletics. Perhaps the only way that I could survive in a world where everybody thought I didn't matter was to have a very fertile imagination, and did I ever. I imagined myself becoming a star quarterback like Kenny Stabler for the Oakland Raiders. I mean, he was left-handed, just like me. Clearly, I was destined to become the next big quarterback.

So I was all fired up for my first PE class. I imagined that I would stroll into the gym and be the best one there. This is where reality and delusional fantasy collided. I couldn't have imagined anything quite like what was about to happen to me and my dream of being an athlete. We were supposed to change from our street clothes into PE outfits. If we didn't, I was informed, our grades would be lowered. I hadn't even known that we would get graded in PE. I thought we would just show up and play; I didn't know we had to dress for class. Not only did we have to dress for PE, but we had to undress first.

This day was getting worse by the second. I was supposed to go into the locker room with a bunch of boys and change my clothes? No frickin' way. The last thing I wanted was any attention, and I was pretty sure that if I had to change my clothes in front of the others I would get a whole lot of attention, and none of it good. At that age, the last thing I wanted was to look stupid in front of a locker room full of my peers.

At the time, my self-perception was that I had a big nose, big feet, and a pipe-cleaner thin body. I was brutally skinny, with little muscle definition, and because I was so skinny I always wore clothes that covered my entire body. This meant that I was basically... sheet white. So a skinny, pasty white boy with a great big nose and overlarge feet getting naked. What a visual.

Then I realized that I didn't have any gym clothes. Yay! I was saved. I would just go over and sit with the rest of the non-suits. But to my horror and dismay, a PE teacher walked up to me and said, "Here's an extra T-shirt and shorts you can use for the day. This is your locker number and your lock. Go change. You got five minutes." This teacher was expecting me to do something—not just one thing, but a bunch of stuff—with a time limit. *Tick, tock, tick, tock.*

I now know that part of my dyslexia is not being able to multitask under pressure. I started to sweat and couldn't breathe. I had no idea what to do. I finally got up, took the combination lock, and looked for my locker. I had never been in a locker room before. It was a maze of tall gray lockers with long benches running between them, and it smelled like old socks and sweat. There were boys everywhere, changing, slamming the locker doors, yelling at the top of their lungs, and running around. This locker room was an absolute out-of-control zoo.

I looked at my combination lock and realized I had no idea how to use it. The combination was written on the piece of paper attached to the lock: L36-R10-L16. The letters and numbers started to jump around, and I wasn't even sure what 'L' and 'R' stood for. It looked like everyone else knew how to use their locks, and I didn't want to be the only one who didn't know what he was doing. I was considering running out of the gym when Steve, my classmate from English, passed by and said, "Let's go, man; roll call is in four minutes."

I decided not to use my lock because I didn't want to be late. I was also trying to figure out how I could change from my street clothes into PE clothes without anyone seeing me naked. I put my jacket and books in the locker and thought if I just waited long enough, everybody would leave. No such luck. Then I had the great idea to change in the bathroom stall. Problem solved! Except, when I came out and went back to my locker... all my stuff was gone. So began my first day in PE class.

Nowadays, expectations of a PE class are a little different. Generally speaking, they're more lax. In the '60s, there were skills that you were expected to master by the time you graduated from eighth grade. In the classroom I had no such expectations—just be quiet and stay out of trouble and I would pass. I liked being in the Shadows. I was done trying to find my area of expertise in that space. I had none and I didn't expect to develop any. There was only one class standing in my way. You would expect it to be English, math, or maybe history. Nope; the class that stood in the way of my escape from junior high was physical education.

PE required Skills Tests. I didn't know what they were, and as it turned out, these Skills Tests were my worst nightmare. It was one thing to suck at something—I mean, to suck *really bad*—but it was even worse to suck at something in front of your whole class. Public and humiliating... great. Just like the Spelling Bee.

You took a skill like rope climbing, added a time limit—*tick, tock, tick, tock*—and a captive audience, and there you go: public humiliation. This particular test required the student (or, some might say, victim) to climb up a rope to the top of the gym rafters and ring a bell. Your climb time was your score.

That didn't seem too hard. I loved to climb trees, so how much harder could it be to climb a rope? Our gym teacher even demonstrated special techniques for climbing. Unfortunately, all these techniques required some semblance of upper body strength. "If you can do ten push-ups, you should be okay," my teacher said. Ten push-ups? I could do three push-ups, and then a bunch of push-downs (lying on my face, ha ha). It was quickly becoming clear that my opinion of my own athletic prowess was highly overinflated.

Our class sat in a circle around the suspended rope. I waited among the group as we watched one student at a time struggle to reach the top of the rope and ring the bell. Some kids made it up in less than one minute; others took two, three, and even four minutes, but they all made it in the end.

Then it was my turn.

All eyes were on me, but I didn't care. I had a plan. My dad once told me "slow and steady wins the race." If I took my time and worked my way up gradually, I could make it. I blew on my hands and started up the rope. After about seven or eight pulls, I had gotten only about six feet off the ground, with about six more to go. I thought to myself, *My plan is working; I can do this...*" until I tried to take another pull on the rope, my arms started shaking, and I didn't go anywhere.

I tried again, with the same results. I struggled to move my arms and legs for what seemed like three days with no success. I just hung there, shaking. One of the kids yelled out, "Hey! He looks like a tea bag, just hanging around." Everybody laughed. I didn't want to be laughed at, or be that strange kid who couldn't do anything, so with anger and the desire to fit in burning in my heart, I tried again. I was determined to keep moving up the rope, but my body had other plans. When I let go with one hand to grab higher up on the rope, my other hand also let go, and down I went. Six feet never seemed so far, and 125 pounds never made as much noise as I did when I hit the mat, flat on my back.

And that, my friends, is how you flunk a Skills Test.

There was a gap between my high IQ and low academic scores, and I could tell that this gap was widening, even in PE. Why couldn't I remember my combination? Why did I think it was only okay to change in the bathroom stall? And why couldn't I pass a stupid Skills Test? I was stuck between a rock and a rock, with no way of getting out.

So far in my schooling I hadn't encountered too many teachers who weren't completely frustrated by my inability to grasp the material that they were presenting. But that all changed in junior high. Mr. Ball and Mr. Nielson were two of the PE teachers on staff. Although I didn't have either of them as my instructors, I always saw them around the gym or the field, and we crossed paths in other ways.

When I couldn't figure out how to use my combination lock, Mr. Ball got me a padlock. When I kept getting my stuff stolen from the locker room because I wouldn't change in front of the other boys, Mr. Nielson let me suit up in an empty part of the locker room. They helped me whenever they saw me struggling with physical skills such as bar dips, the ladder climb, sit-ups, or push-ups. This reassurance that there were people who cared about me and who were also teachers was a new and very important experience for me. But it wasn't until the end of my eighth-grade year that I realized how important and life changing their support was going to be.

The rumor was well established at my school: if you didn't pass eighth grade PE, you had to come back and repeat it the following year. That meant coming back during high school and making up a junior high PE class as a ninth grader. I couldn't imagine doing that, but with only six weeks left in the school year, I needed to make up 65 points to get a C- in PE. Holy crap!

One day as I was leaving the gym at the end of my class, Mr. Ball came up to me and asked me how I was doing. I told him that I wasn't going to pass eighth grade PE because I was 65 points behind, and that I would see him the next year. He looked at me and said, "How would you like to make up those 65 points?"

"How?" I asked. "There are only six weeks left in the quarter, and I've flunked every skill test I've ever taken."

"You can run them off. One lap for every point," replied Mr. Ball.

I thought to myself, *"65 laps? Really!?"* I know this is going to come as a shock, but I sucked at running too.

Then something happened that I didn't expect at all. "Listen, Scott," said Mr. Ball. "I'll make you a deal. You come and meet me on the track every day after school, and I'll teach you how to run." And he did.

When I began running, I could barely do a single lap. I breathed heavily and felt like throwing up after one turn around the track. I didn't know how to pace myself or how to use proper running form. I just shot straight off the starting line at full blast, and would be cramping up and suffering before I reached the first turn. All the while, my arms flapped and danced in the breeze, looking nothing like a serious runner's.

Each day I would show up after school, and there was Mr. Ball waiting for me on the dusty track. We worked on my form and my pacing, and a month later I was able to run four laps without stopping or throwing up.

I put in the effort, but he put in the time—a new concept for me. He expected something from me: he expected me to do my best, and then some. After four weeks, I had run 72 laps and earned a C for my eighth grade PE class. This was the first grade I felt like I had actually earned, and I was extremely proud of it.

When I left to go to high school, I had no intentions of ever returning to my junior high to visit. It took six years, and a lot of water under the bridge, but I did come back eventually because, as it turns out, one teacher can save your life.

Sounding a bit agitated and exasperated, Grace asked, "Okay, so junior high school sucked too, I get it. But what about high school? Were you good at anything? Ever!?"

"Wow, Grace, that's harsh! You don't have to be sooo rude, Mr. D was just—"

"I'm not being rude, just honest. Until I got here, my school experience sucked too. What I want to know is, how did you get through it if you were terrible at everything?"

13.

DREAMS CAN COME TRUE

My fantasy life had never lived up to my real life. I fantasized about being:

- A star football player. *Didn't happen.*
- An academic superstar. *Nope.*
- An all-around heartthrob. *Yeah right.*
- A drummer in the marching band. *Yes!* But it almost didn't happen.

At Berkeley High School, any student interested in joining the band had to try out. This took me by surprise, since I thought all I would have to do was sign up and show up. And not only did you have to try out, but there were two different parts to these tryouts: one for playing an instrument, and another for marching.

To me, the word "tryout" meant "taking a test," so I was understandably worried that my dream was going to be over before it ever started. The musical audition required you to be able to read music and play with your section. My section was percussion. I had been playing snare drum since I was in third grade, but was never able to read the sheet music. I compensated by listening to the music, getting to know the rhythms and styles, and then playing along with it. I didn't know this at the time, but I am a *kinesthetic learner*. I must physically experience something for it to connect and stick.

The song we auditioned with was "Stars and Stripes" by John Phillip Sousa. Before the tryouts, I listened to the music at home and played along with it. I practiced the rhythms everywhere I went. No, I didn't tote my drum kit all around town; I heard the music in my head and played the drums with my hands on my legs, and spoons on the table, and drumsticks on a phonebook.

Thanks to all this practice, by the time of the audition I was comfortable and ready. When it was our turn to play as a unit, I followed the other drummers and did fine. When it was time for me to play solo, I played loud and proud. Because I knew this style of music, was flashy, and played with confidence, I did a good enough job to pass the musical section of the tryouts.

But the tryouts also involved marching, and the thought of that brought up flashbacks of my disastrous beginnings as a crossing guard in fifth grade. The way I saw it, I could blend in as one of the six drummers, but if I tried marching in formation in a highly choreographed routine, one false move could destroy the whole thing. As much as I wanted to be a part of this band, I certainly didn't want to stand out as the only band member who did not know his left from his right, or be laughed at for forgetting a formation or doing the wrong routine. It sure didn't look this hard in *The Music Man*.

The evening before the marching tryouts, I told my mother that I was not going to go out for band after all. She looked really confused. "I thought that this was a lifelong dream of yours," she said. "Why stop when you're so close?"

I considered declaring that being in marching band was not cool or that I didn't care anymore, but I knew she would see right through that lie. "Tomorrow's tryout is marching, and I know I'm going to mess up," I confessed. "I want to be in marching band so bad, but I'm just not smart enough to remember everything."

I knew that saying I wasn't smart enough would probably set my mother off, but instead she just sat there in the kitchen, thinking and not saying a word. Finally, she said, "That's too bad; I was looking forward to watching you march in parades and at football games." Then she got up and left the room.

I was floored. My mother wasn't mad at me? She was *disappointed* in me? I followed her into the living room, intending to justify my reasons for not trying out, but when I got there she was sitting at the dining room table by herself. In the center of the table she had placed half a dozen spoons in a pile.

I sat down next to her. But instead of playing our old family game, she took one of the spoons and rapped me on my knuckles with it. Looking directly at me, she said firmly, "We don't quit in this family. I know you want this, so figure it out." Standing up, my mother continued, "Scott, don't give up on your dream just because you're scared. We all get scared at times. Figure this out. Come up with a plan like you did when you were in the crossing guard. But don't you give up, because if you do you will regret it for the rest of your life." And with that, she left the room for the second time in less than five minutes.

I was stunned. Not only was my mother disappointed in me, but I had never heard her use the word "regret" before. This was totally out of character for my mom. She wasn't giving up on me, but for the first time in my life she walked out—and, in doing so, made sure I had to come up with a solution on my own. Whether I was going to give up or try out for the marching band was totally up to me. Sink or swim, the ball was in my court. I wasn't sure what to think or what to do, so I just sat there with my hands on top of the pile of spoons. What did she mean when she had said, "...like you did when you were in the crossing guard?"

After what seemed like hours of racking my brain, I finally realized what my mother meant. I needed to develop a strategy and figure out how to survive the marching part of the tryouts without making a total fool of myself. I knew that I could not rely on knowing my left from my right under pressure, or on being able to memorize a complicated marching routine on the spot. I tried to think of ways to hide my weaknesses and follow the others while marching. Maybe I could write "left" and "right" on my hands or on my drum? But neither this nor any of the other strategies I could think of seemed like they would work.

The longer I contemplated this problem the more frustrated I became. I absently picked up a couple of spoons and started tapping them on the pile of other spoons, softly at first and then with more force. Spoons began flying everywhere as I got more creative, knocking them around, making up tricks and rhythms, and just having a lot of fun.

"Why couldn't the marching band be fun like this?" I thought. Then it occurred to me that I was worrying about all the things that I was not good at: reading sheet music and memorizing complicated routines. I had completely forgotten about what had attracted me to the marching band in the first place: performing.

By this time, I knew my weaknesses quite well, but I had forgotten all about any strengths I might have. I didn't think I had too many talents, but performing was one of my strong points. If I had been asked to describe myself at this point in time, I would have used words like "flawed," "defective," "failure," "weak link," "Achilles' heel," and so on. Finding words to describe my positive attributes was much harder for me. Instead of describing myself as having a skill, specialty, aptitude, or talent, I would spin things negatively: I was "lucky," or it was a "fluke" or an "accident" that I was successful at something.

The one thing that I could rely on was being able to perform. I decided that I would try out the next day, and that I would "be a performer" when I auditioned. *Go big or go home* would be my mantra from this point forward.

The next day when I took to the field, I marched and played my heart out. When I made a wrong turn or played at an incorrect time, instead of acting like I made a mistake, I went big and performed like the marching band was the most important thing in the world to me—which it was. I was the biggest, loudest, most exaggerated marcher of them all. When the audition was over and I had left the field, I expected the crowd to laugh. Instead, the Drum Major came up to me and said, "You're the first freshman who actually looks like you're having fun. I think you'll be a crowd favorite."

After all my worrying, I made the marching band on my first try, and for the first time I thought about myself as having strengths, not just weaknesses. Being a member of my high school marching band was a highlight of my high school experience. If I hadn't tried out, I would have had very little reason to continue in high school. It was at this time that I began thinking about how to solve problems using my strengths, as opposed to always thinking I wasn't good enough.

The first time that I publicly performed with the marching band was at a football game. When we marched out onto the field, it felt just like I had always imagined it would. For the first time in my life, one of my dreams had come true. I remember telling my mother how happy I was that I didn't quit. She said that she was proud of me for figuring out how to solve the problems of the tryouts. Then she looked at me with a twinkle in her eye and said, "I wonder what else you can do?"

"Wow!!" Grace blurted out. "Your mom sounds cool. It seems like she really understood what you were going through. I wish my parents understood me like that."

"Besides the marching band, was there anything else in high school that you became good at?" asked James.

14.

PAIN, SWEAT, AND AGONY

When my senior year in high school finally rolled around, I did something completely out of character: I tried out for the cross-country team. My friend Eric was going to try out, so I thought, "What the heck? What's the worst that could happen?" I wouldn't make the team? Big deal. On the other hand, I figured that if I did make the team, I would get a uniform to wear around school... and maybe, just maybe, girls would notice me.

Eric was a sophomore while I was a senior—a nineteen-year-old senior. He ended up making the Jr. Varsity team, and I made the Reserves. What I didn't know was that the Reserve team was for runners who couldn't make any of the other teams. The teams were broken into levels in descending order: Varsity, Junior Varsity, Frosh-Soph, Freshmen, and then (last and probably least) Reserve.

I didn't care where I placed, though. The point was, I had made the team, and I was proud of that. It was the first time in my life that I had teammates.

Our initial off-campus workout was also the first time in my life that I ran more than two miles without stopping. We started out with the others on the team, but that only lasted until we got to the bottom of the hill at Marin Street. This hill went straight up, and we were supposed to run up it? My family didn't even *drive* up this hill because it was so steep.

Eric and I started up. It wasn't as bad as I thought it was going to be for a block or two, but then it started really getting steep. By this time, I had turned into a six-foot ball of sweat and snot. The asphalt pounded back up through my feet and lower legs. With each thud of rubber and road, endless beads of sweat, like so many fleas leaping off the back of a just-bathed dog, flew in thousands of directions. My lungs burned, and my legs ached. Finally, through a combination of jogging, walking, and crawling, I reached the top of Marin Street where Eric was waiting. I was no longer so sure being on the team was worth the pain and agony that I had just endured.

Trying to catch my breath, I looked at Eric and asked, "Now that we're finished with our run, how do we get back to school?"

I wasn't sure if I could even walk back to school, but Eric smiled at me and said, "We're not done, we haven't even gotten to the field where we're supposed to meet the coach to start our workout. This is just the warm-up, Scott."

"People do this for *fun*?" I wheezed, incredulous.

When we finally got to the field, the coach was waiting in his car.

"What took you so long?" he demanded. "Everybody else has already started practice."

Two hours later, after running around the perimeter of Tilden Park in the Berkeley Hills, Eric and I finally arrived back at school in the dark. I was so sore and tired I could barely change my clothes. As we walked home and joked about my first day of practice, I realized that, no matter how painful this was, I was sharing it with a friend, and I was finally on a team.

When the first meet of the season arrived, we went to another school to participate. We had to compete in five separate races. Eric ran in the second race while I had to wait until the fifth and final race. I was very nervous because I had never run in a race before, and I wasn't sure what my strategy should be. I asked my coach, and do you want to know what his advice was? "Run fast!" Wow, why didn't I think of that?

Run fast, he said... so I did. When the race started, I took off as fast as I could. I ran for about a quarter mile, until my lungs began to burn and it was becoming hard for me to breathe. I wasn't sure what was going on; I thought that maybe I was dying.

As the race continued, we ran past the crowd of spectators, which included the other runners on my team. Eric yelled at me, "Slow down; you're going too fast!" Going too fast? I thought the coach told me to run fast, and that's what I was trying to do. "Pace yourself," he called after me, "you have a mile and a half left!"

I had forgotten about pacing and what Mr. Ball had taught me. Wait a second, did he say I had a mile and a half left? Just when all this new information was circling through my mind, we came to a turn in the road—and there, right in front of me, like the Great Wall of China, was this giant hill rising up from the ground and reaching into the sky.

Holy COW! Who would build a race track on a mountain resembling Marin Street? What kind of sadistic sport was this? Halfway up the hill I started to walk (well, actually it was more like crawling and climbing). I had never felt pain in my shins, thighs, the backs of my legs, lungs, abdomen, shoulders, arms, and kidneys like this before, and all I wanted was for the pain to stop.

I looked up and I could see the top of the hill. I just wanted to get to the top and get this nightmare over with. Why would anyone do this on purpose? I don't know how I managed, but I eventually reached the top. I looked down and saw the finish line, but I didn't see any of the other runners ahead of me. Where did they go? Hadn't I just been following them? Then I heard someone yell, "Run, dummy! You're in first place!"

How could that be? I had walked up most of that hill. Sure enough, though, I stood upon the summit in first place—but not for long, because when I stopped to look back down the hill, I saw the other runners were catching up, and quickly. Two guys passed on either side of me, and then I heard the cheers encouraging me to start running again, so I took off after the others.

We were the last race of the day, and most of the bystanders and other runners had already gone home. Even so, we gave it all we had as we pounded toward the finish line. We put on a great finale, and to my surprise I came in second. Then my teammates came up to me to congratulate me on my run. I had never felt so bad and so good at the same time. Unbeknownst to me, running would be my gateway into college.

Feigning ignorance, James asked, "What's a gateway, Mr. D? Is it like a portal to another world?" Grinning, James waited for me to continue as Grace rolled her eyes.

15.

COLLEGE

There was a coach from the local community college who had seen me run cross country in high school and thought I had the potential to be a college runner. Now, college was not something that I had planned on doing. I got out of high school qualifying at about a third-grade academic level, and in the back of my mind I thought that college was only for smart people.

I worked that summer doing odd jobs—*really* odd jobs. Because I had a hard time filling out applications due to my poor spelling, my dad helped me get work that nobody else wanted. I unloaded tuna fish boats, built floats, worked security, and even cleaned the local morgue. Since all these jobs required skills that I didn't really possess, I kept bouncing from one job to the next. So, when September came around and I still had the opportunity to go to college, I jumped in with both feet.

My first day on a college campus was an absolute blast. I went to Alameda Junior College, an institution that was in the middle of nowhere. As runners, we were big fish in a little pond. To be sure, I was not a student, and I didn't come to school to be a student. I came to school to run, and I wasn't even sure I could do that. Track and field was a big deal at this school. The team had won state championships, which meant there were high standards for me to live up to.

On the first day of practice I got to meet my new coach, Eddie Hart, who was a gold medal Olympic runner. In high school there were a lot of cross-country runners, probably about forty in all. But here at Alameda Junior College, there were only three serious cross-country runners on the team. I had gone from being barely noticed as a runner in high school to a member of a very visible team, and now the pressure was on. One of the veteran runners, Barry Smith, was a short guy with a whole lot of hair. He didn't talk much at first, but as the season went on we became close friends.

About three weeks into the season, Barry ran up to me after practice.

"Hey Scott, I noticed your times are faster than mine, but when we run against each other you never beat me. Do you know why?"

"No, I just thought you were better than me when it comes to the actual race."

"Well, I think I might know. I think your head is getting in the way."

"My head? What do you mean?" I asked.

Barry explained, "Coach says that running is ninety percent mental and ten percent physical. He says the hardest part of being an athlete is the mental portion, not the physical one, and that your mind can get in the way and psych you out when you're running and over-thinking everything."

"Huh?"

"It's hard for me to explain, but I can show you. Do you have extra time right now?"

"Sure."

"Great. Let's race a mile, and I want you to run behind me and count the words on the back of my shirt. You can only pass me when you're confident you've counted the correct number of words. I know how many words there are, so if you pass me and have counted wrong, I win."

"You're on!" I said.

And with that, we were off. I ran on Barry's outside shoulder and started counting. I focused with all my might on counting while we both ran at top speeds. The funny thing was I stopped thinking about everything else, except the words. I was not aware of any other sights or sounds on the track. I counted over and over, never getting the same number twice, so I focused harder on trying to slow my breathing and quiet my mind. Suddenly Barry stepped off the track, breaking my trance.

"Go, Scott, go!" he yelled.

I had half a lap to go and an abundance of energy left, so I pushed harder and finished strong. As I was catching my breath, I looked around for Barry. He was walking over to me from the other side of the track and checking his stopwatch.

"What was that all about?" I demanded. "Why did you stop?"

"I couldn't go any farther," he said, holding up his stopwatch. "You just ran a 4:09 mile. Isn't that your best time by 11 seconds?"

"What?" I couldn't believe it. "I didn't think we were going that fast."

Barry smiled. "See, ninety percent mental."

I learned two things in junior college, and I didn't learn them in a classroom. I learned what it meant to be a teammate, and—thanks to Barry's friendship and guidance—I learned what it took to be an athlete. I ran cross-country and track and field for two years. I was a pretty good runner, made a close friend, developed confidence in my running, and felt I was ready for the next step in my athletic and academic career: I was ready to go to a four-year college.

At least, I thought I was.

"That's really awesome, Mr. D," said James. "You found the one thing that you could do really well, and that got you through college. I love a happy ending." He thought for a few seconds. "This is an example of the dyslexic spirit prevailing. All you needed was a chance to show the world who you were, a track star."

Ignoring James, Grace asked, "Which university did you go to, Mr. D?"

I grew up in Berkeley, California. My mother and sister had attended the University of California, Berkeley ("Cal" for short), so when it came time for me to choose a four-year college, I wanted to go there too. I was a pretty good junior college mile runner, and there were some small colleges that were very interested in having me run track for them, but I paid no attention to any of their offers. I was convinced that the only legitimate choice for me was to go to Cal.

The word *legitimate* was very important to me at this point in my life, and I felt I had a lot to prove to the world and to myself. Those small schools that had expressed an interest in me were not *legitimate* schools in my eyes. I had to go to Cal to prove to everybody that they had been wrong about me. I wasn't *stupid*, *dumb*, *lazy*, *retarded*, or any of the other names they had called me. I wasn't the *scarecrow* or the *teabag* anymore. I was going to prove to all those people who didn't believe in me how wrong they were, and I was going to do all this by going to Cal and becoming a track star.

That was my dream and my reality, because in my head I thought that attending Cal would be just as easy and welcoming as my junior college experience had been. The real issue, however, was that the only person who needed proof of my self-worth was me. I needed validation from the outside world because I truly didn't believe I was worth it on the inside.

I entered Cal as a junior college transfer. My grades were average, somewhere around a 2.5 GPA, and just good enough to keep me eligible to run. I had attended classes during my junior college years, but I didn't recall ever needing to study hard or ask for help. They didn't really ask you to do anything, so it was fairly easy, and I thought that it would be the same at Cal. I would be able to run as well as attend class. The concept of being a real student with real academic skills was not a concern of mine. Boy, was I in for a rude awakening. All I really wanted to do was become a Pac-10 track star and beat Stanford, but I never got that chance.

When I started school at Cal I had to decide on a major, so I picked Political Science. It sounded cool, but I didn't really know what political science was. Having a major wasn't all that important to me; I was in school to run. For the first time, I had found something I was good at and I wanted to keep doing it. I didn't think it was too unreasonable to assume that I could keep running and going to school, and nothing would change.

But change, as it turns out, is what life is all about... and my life was just about to start getting interesting. After attending school for about two weeks, I thought everything was going well. I went to practice every day. But now I was a small fish in a big pond. The coach and most of my teammates didn't even know my name, but that was all right with me. I was running, and I had a pretty good shot at making the team.

On the academic front, though, things were a little different. I attended classes, I watched and listened to the teachers, and I even read the books... but I had no idea what they were talking about. I would go into the library, pull out the book I was to study from, read a chapter, and then try to figure out what I had just read and what it meant. But no matter how many times I reread a chapter, it still made no sense. I had no idea why I couldn't figure out the material. And when I listened to the professors giving lectures in the giant lecture halls, all I heard was incomprehensible noise. I didn't know what to do, and I didn't want to tell anyone I was having such a hard time because I was ashamed.

One of the classes I took was Statistics. From my perspective, it was just a lot of fancy math; I had no idea what the class was about. Whenever the teacher talked, all the students would take notes or nod their heads like they understood what he was saying. But for me it was like he was talking in a foreign language which I could not speak or understand.

The teacher would ask the class if anybody had any questions, but I never raised my hand. Oh, I had questions all right, but I was too ashamed and too afraid to admit to anybody that I couldn't figure out the answers by myself. So I just kept plugging along, looking at the pages that meant nothing to me, listening to words that I didn't understand, and praying to myself that all of a sudden something would click in my head and this crap would all make sense.

Our first Statistics test was terrifying. We were given a hundred questions and provided a long, narrow piece of paper imprinted with a hundred rows of bubbles. I was supposed to read each question on the test and then fill in the correct bubble on the multiple-choice answer sheet. For example, if I thought the answer was option number four, I would fill in the fourth bubble over. This sheet of paper was called a Scantron form.

As I began the test, I started sweating. My ears began ringing, and my mouth was so dry that I couldn't swallow. The room was starting to spin, but I kept on trying to figure out the answers to the questions.

When I finished the test, I looked up and realized I was the only student still in the room. The teacher was looking at me impatiently, so I sheepishly got up, went down to the front of the classroom, and handed him my test. He looked at me and said, "What took you so long? This was the easiest test that I'll be giving this semester."

I looked at him with a horrified stare. If this was the easiest test of the semester, then I was in serious trouble.

"Do you understand this material?" he asked. "Do you need extra help?"

Extra help! Why would he think I needed extra help? He hadn't even corrected my test yet. *"He must think I'm stupid."*

I looked at him and said, "No, thank you. I get it. I understand this material." And then I turned and walked out of his classroom. I could not admit to him or to myself that I was way over my head, and sinking fast.

The following week we got our tests back, and I had scored twenty out of a hundred. It was the second lowest score in the class. Well, there it was: reality biting me in the butt again. For the two years I was at Alameda I felt like a college student, but at Cal reality finally caught up with me. I was dumb as a post, and I knew it. Within a week I was no longer eligible to practice with the cross-country team, and I had to prove myself academically before I could return.

I was in a tailspin. Not sure of what to do, I just kept on trying, and continued hitting my head against the wall. I couldn't understand why things weren't coming to me, and by the time the second test in Statistics rolled around I had all but given up. I walked into the classroom completely defeated. As I took my seat, I noticed a girl one row below and to the right of me. She was sitting in a position that enabled me to look down her shirt. (By this time my focus was no longer on school but on just about everything else.)

When I got my test, I started filling out the Scantron sheet, just guessing at all the answers. Then I realized that I was no longer looking down the pretty girl's shirt; I was looking at her answer sheet. I had never cheated on a test in my life until that moment. But I no longer cared. Besides, I reasoned, how much help was cheating going to be? Maybe I would get thirty out of a hundred instead of twenty. Big flipping deal.

So, without even trying to disguise what I was doing, I started copying her answers. When I was finished, I realized that I had copied every last one of her answers, so I erased a few marks and changed them. In my head, I figured I didn't want my score to be identical to hers. I turned in my answer sheet and headed home.

By the time our next class rolled around, I'd almost forgotten about the test. Cheating or not, I knew I didn't belong in school. But I sat down to wait while the teacher handed out the test results. He passed back all the tests except for mine, and every time he walked by he would smile at me. This freaked me out; why wasn't he giving me my test? Then our teacher took his place in front of the class and began to talk.

"I started teaching to make a difference, but I rarely do. I want to motivate my students to do better, but I rarely have. So it gives me great pride to announce the highest score, and the biggest turnaround on a test score that I have ever seen."

I still didn't know why he hadn't given me my test. Maybe he forgot; cool. I didn't need the embarrassment anyway.

"Scott, would you please stand up," the teacher said.

"Oh, no!" I thought. *"He's going to kick me out of his class right now."* I slowly stood up to face the music.

"Scott, I'm so very proud of you. You went from worst to first. You scored 20% on the first test you took, but this time you scored 98% and best in the class." And with that, he came up to my chair and handed me my test.

"Thank you." If my response were any more sheepish, it could have joined a herd.

"No, thank *you*. I'm just glad I was able to motivate you to do your best."

Then the whole class clapped. Not only did cheating help my grade, now this teacher thought that he had helped turn me around. Boy, what had I done?

While walking home that evening, I couldn't help but feel guilty. I had cheated, and gotten away with it. I should be happy and relieved, but I wasn't. When I got home I told my mother what had happened. I figured she'd be mad and disappointed in me, which I expected, and felt I deserved. After I told her the story, though, she started to laugh.

She asked me, "How did you get a better score than the person you cheated off of?" And then she laughed again.

Wow. I asked my mother what I should do, and she told me to follow my heart and do the right thing. The right thing? What was the right thing to do? If I didn't say anything, I would still know I cheated, but if I did say something I would probably flunk the class and disappoint the teacher.

I wanted my mom to tell me what to do, but she just said it was up to me and that no matter what I did, she would be proud. Damn. I was twenty-two years old, still living at home, and I relied on my mother for emotional support and guidance. And what did I get? Zip, zero, nada. I was on my own.

Up until this point, I thought that all learning was done in the classroom. I was starting to realize that learning and growing happened any time you let it. Even when things were bad, like they were right then, you could still learn from the experience. So, what was I going to learn from this? Whatever it was, I realized that it was going to be up to me. Great, I thought, I get to teach myself.

The next time I had my Statistics class, I went up to the teacher after class to confess my sins.

"Dr. Pilard, do you have a second?"

Looking up from his notes, he responded, "For my *star* student, of course."

"About that, Dr. Pilard... I have something I need to tell you."

"What's that?"

"I... I... cheated on the last test."

The expression on his face turned to one of betrayal. He looked really hurt. He didn't thank me for telling the truth; in fact, I think he was sorry I had told the truth. I realized that he had really thought that he had turned me around, and now that he knew I had cheated, it took away his feeling of success. I was trying to do the right thing, but I was still hurting someone. He changed my grade to an F, which I deserved.

Rules were not as stringent in the 1970s as they are today. Cal didn't haul me before the Dean of Students and summarily eject me from the institution. But I did learn something from the experience. I learned that being a man meant accepting the consequences of your actions. At least I had learned one lesson, if not the one the class was all about.

After two quarters, I flunked out of Cal with a 1.1 GPA. The worst part of my failure, though, was that I didn't get to run track—which, as I've mentioned, was the only reason I attended school. I concluded that I had nowhere to go. Even though I wasn't a competent student, I'd truly believed that my athletic ability would get me through school. My feelings, of course, were not rooted in any kind of reality. I truly believed that attending Cal would validate who I was, and transform me into a legitimate person with worthwhile, admirable, high-profile, and respectable goals.

So when I flunked out of school I felt exposed. People could see me now for who I really was: that slow, dumb, retarded kid who didn't fit in anywhere and couldn't do anything well. How low is low? I was so far down, I would have needed to climb the stairs and then take an elevator up a few more floors just to reach the depths of despair. I felt my life was over. I had no prospects, no dreams, and no desire.

"Wow, Mr. D... that story's really heartbreaking. I thought all of your failures were behind you." James sighed.

"I have a question, Mr. D. You said you were a political science major in college; when did you study acting?" asked Grace.

16.

No Small Parts, Just Small Actors

Back in high school I had always wanted to be in a school play, but I was deathly afraid of auditions. By my senior year, though, I had built up the courage to audition for the spring production, *The Madwoman of Chaillot*. The director, Mr. Coffey, told me that I needed to prepare a three-minute monologue to perform in front of him, the assistant directors, and all the students who were trying out. He told me that the monologue could be from a play or a book, but it needed to be in the style of the type of character I wanted to play. He also said that I had to be off-book for the audition. I nodded that I understood his instructions and left... but I had no idea what he was talking about.

I started to panic as I walked the halls of my high school. Then I ran into Carolyn, a friend from marching band. She took one look at me and asked what was wrong. I had a good relationship with Carolyn, as we had also been in the crossing guard together in elementary school. I knew she had participated in theater in junior high, and thought maybe she could help me make sense of what Mr. Coffey had told me.

"I want to try out for the school play," I told her, "but I don't know what 'character style,' 'monologue,' or 'off-book' mean." She smiled and explained the whole thing to me as we walked together.

"Character style," she said, "means the type of person you want to play." She stopped and looked directly into my eyes. "Do you want to be a heartthrob or be laughed at?" Well, that was an easy one. At that time in my life I saw myself as the brooding, smoldering, and dangerous leading-man type, like Marlon Brando or James Dean.

So that was character type, but what was "off-book?" Off-book, Carolyn explained, meant that you had to have the monologue memorized, and a monologue, I discovered, was just one person talking. So all I had to do was find a speech that fit the time requirements, had a beginning, middle, and end, and contained a problem and its solution. I figured if I focused on the monologue as a story it would make more sense to me, and then I would have a better chance of remembering it. But how would I find something like that? Both of my parents were writers, but I wanted to solve this problem on my own—after all, I was a senior.

I decided to go to the local library. Once there, I explained my predicament to the librarian, Miss Robinson. She looked at me for a few seconds and then told me to wait for a moment. Ten minutes later she came back with a book of monologues, with one already picked out.

"This monologue will be perfect for you," she explained. "It's about an old man who lived his whole life on a deserted island, and when he could no longer take the isolation and solitude, decided to end it all by filling his pockets full of rocks and walking into the ocean."

She smiled and waited for my reaction. I was excited; it seemed clear to me that the monologue would land me a lead romantic part in the play. Perfect! The world would see me for who I really was: a James Dean heartthrob type. There wouldn't be a dry eye in the house. (Well, I was right about that last part, at least).

I checked the book out and took it home. I decided to try to memorize my monologue by reading and rereading it out loud until it stuck. "The sky is so blue and filled with birds. The water so plentiful, brimming with sea life. This should be my paradise; instead, it's my inferno... The sky is so blue and filled with birds. The water so plentiful, brimming with sea life. This should be my paradise; instead, it's my inferno."

After about an hour of rehearsing, I closed the book and tried to recite the lines without looking. Nothing came to me. I couldn't remember what I had just spent an hour reading, over and over. I tried it again, with the same results.

I was just about to give up when I remembered the play my mother had written for us when I was in first grade. She hadn't given me any lines in the script because she wanted me to react to the other actors. She wanted me to *improvise*. I had managed to do that, and the play turned out great, so maybe I didn't need to memorize these lines. How was I going to react to others, though, if I was the only one on stage? Then it hit me: I could react to the *situation*.

So I took my monologue, went to the neighborhood park, and found a secluded area. I wanted to put myself into this man's shoes. I wanted to know what it would feel like if I was in his place, isolated and alone with no hope of rescue. I stood on a small rock formation and pretended it was an island, and I had nowhere to go and no one to talk to. I began to experience despair, sadness, eventually even depression.

"Why, God, have you forgotten me!?" I blurted out, surprising myself. "I have no one, not even you... there is no point for me to continue on; it would be easier for me to die than to keep on living." Wow! I had put myself into this man's shoes and the monologue had started to flow. Not word for word, but close enough. More importantly, I felt this man's emotions. I became him. Isn't that what acting is? So for the next two days I returned to the park, stood on that rock formation, and became that old man, reciting my lines to no one.

When the day of the audition arrived, I felt prepared and relaxed. I could remember most of my lines, and I even decided to bring some rocks, so I could put them in my pockets at the end of the scene. I entered the rehearsal hall to find a small temporary stage set up on one side of the room, with fifty folding chairs facing the stage. The auditioning actors, director, and assistant director would sit there. There were no stage lights, sets, or even curtains.

When it was my turn to audition, I walked up to the stage full of confidence. I felt like I was going to blow Mr. Coffey away with my emotional power and strength. Keep in mind that I had never taken an acting lesson in my life. I turned to face my audience, introduced myself, and waited for my direction.

"Thank you, Scott. Please begin when you are ready."

Once I got started, I felt totally into the character that I was playing, and I gave it all I had. As I went through my audition piece, I gestured to the sky and the ocean, baring my soul for all to see. I noticed that some of the audience members were laughing. The more exaggerated and emotional I got, the more people in the audience started to laugh.

When I finally got to the end of my monologue, put my rocks into my pockets, and pretended to walk into the ocean and drown, the audience was in hysterics. Some were laughing, some were crying from laughing too much, and others had fallen into the aisles. When I was done, I noticed that everyone in the room was clapping for me while they were laughing at me. But I didn't *want* them to laugh at me. I had just recited a monologue about a man wanting to die... and they were laughing?

Then I began to cry. I was so embarrassed, I just wanted to die. Mr. Coffey tried to talk to me, but he was still laughing too hard. Panicking, I jumped off the stage and ran through the audience, out of the rehearsal hall, and all the way home.

When I got home, I told my mom that I was sick, went upstairs to bed, and cried myself to sleep. I stayed home in bed for the next two days because I was too embarrassed to show my face at school. On the second evening that I had stayed home, I got a phone call from Carolyn. She sounded worried.

"Are you okay?" she asked. "You left the audition so fast the other day."

When I didn't say anything, she continued. "Mr. Coffey is looking for you."

"I bet," I said meekly.

"You got a lead role!"

"A lead?" I was shocked.

"Yes, the lead comedic role. Mr. Coffey told us that you could be the next Jerry Lewis; you were *that* funny."

Something inside me went cold. I was *not* trying to be funny, and Jerry Lewis was a slapstick clown of an actor. I was trying to be dramatic, not comedic. Carolyn congratulated me on earning a lead part on my first try and then hung up.

After playing hooky for two days, I finally went back to school. I avoided the theater at all costs because I was embarrassed that I had run out of the audition. I was also bent out of shape that people thought I was trying to be funny. If I was going to come out of the Shadows and be judged by people, I did not want to be exposed as a clown. I truly felt that being a comedic actor was beneath me, and that it did not take any talent to make people laugh.

A few days later while I was sitting in English class, Mr. Coffey came into the class and asked my teacher if he could talk to me alone for a moment. What did he want? Was he here to laugh at me some more?

"Scott, I just wanted to make sure that you knew that you have earned the main comedic role in our upcoming play. I'm concerned that you don't understand what an honor it is to be cast as a lead."

I squared my shoulders. "Mr. Coffey, I really do not see myself as a comedic actor."

Instead of getting mad, he smiled and said, "Do you think that being a comic actor is easy?" I nodded. "Being funny is one of the hardest things an actor can do. It takes timing, instinct, and showmanship. But most importantly, it takes talent, natural talent." He looked me right in the eyes. "You have a natural, God-given gift. I have never seen such a hilarious audition, even if you weren't trying to be funny. You are a natural. You remind me of a young Dick Van Dyke." He handed me a script. "Review your part, and I will see you this coming Monday after school to start rehearsals." He patted me on my shoulder and then left.

I stood in the hallway, alone and stunned. I had seen *Mary Poppins* and I knew who Dick Van Dyke was—and yes, he was very funny. But what had the most impact on me was that the director thought I had *natural talent*. I was sold. I would be a Dick, not a Jerry.

When I got home that evening, I sat down at my desk in my room and started underlining all my lines just like Mr. Coffey had instructed me. I figured that I might have a few lines, but most of what I was going to do I could make up. I figured that was how it worked, and that the lines were only meant to be suggestions that I would use to develop my character. If not, why would we need a director? The funny thing is that this made perfect sense to me. After I had gone through the two-hundred-page script, I went back and counted my lines. Holy smokes! I had more than thirty lines in the play. I was sure Mr. Coffey had a plan for me.

A few days later, when I arrived at my first practice for the play, I was very excited because I thought, *"This is going to be fun."* Mr. Coffey said I was a natural, so I didn't worry. I had familiarized myself with my lines and character, and I had a lot of ideas to add to the character to make him even funnier. When it was my turn to go onstage, I went up without my script, leaving it in my chair, ready to be funny.

When Mr. Coffey saw that I did not have my script with me he said, "Great, Scott; you're off-book already." Then he told me that I could start.

"Start what?" I asked.

"Start reciting your lines."

"Mr. Coffey, I haven't memorized all my lines yet."

"That's okay, Scott. Get your script, get back onstage, and begin reading your lines out loud."

Out loud and in front of everyone, I thought. Crap... crap... crap.

After one week of trying, I was still no closer to remembering all of my lines. Mr. Coffey started taking them away, one by one, and giving them to the other actors who were in the same scenes. He wanted me to be able to repeat the lines word for word, exactly as they were written. He didn't want me to remove or add anything, just recite from the script. I didn't think this was acting, just regurgitation. No matter how hard I tried to remember the lines, when I got onstage everything went blank.

One day, after a particularly bad rehearsal, Mr. Coffey pulled me aside and informed me that he had given my part to another actor. He said that I could still be in the play, but that I would get a different, smaller part. I was relieved—no memorization, but I would still get to be onstage. As it turned out, my new part had a one-word line, and I was onstage for about two minutes. In a two-hour play, I went from a major role with thirty lines to a two-minute, one-word minor role. But a funny thing happened to me when I stepped onto that stage on opening night: I was bitten by the acting bug.

I wanted to continue my acting career once I got out of high school, so I asked Mr. Coffey if he knew of any drama programs that I could join. He told me that he could do better than that. A friend of his was mounting the San Francisco production of *One Flew Over the Cuckoo's Nest.* He told me that I didn't even need to audition, and that I'd also be paid. Wow, I was going to be a professional actor!

"The only downside is that this part has no lines," he said. Well, that was okay, I thought. I'm just starting out and I'll get bigger parts later.

Mr. Coffey arranged everything for me and told me where to go for my first rehearsal. He handed me the script and instructed me to familiarize myself with it. When he asked if I had heard of this play before and if I knew what a frontal lobotomy was, I hastily assured him that I had this covered and thanked him for all his help.

Now, not only had I *not* heard of this play, I also had *no idea* what a frontal lobotomy was. Back at home, I anxiously read the script and tried to familiarize myself with it, but I had trouble understanding the meaning behind the words. Still, I wasn't too worried because I didn't have any lines, and I assumed all I would have to do was show up and go along with whatever my new director told me to do.

The theater was in San Francisco. It sat around three hundred people, and the coolest thing about it was the giant half circle of a stage. Only about six feet separated it from the front row, so if you were on either side of the stage you could practically touch the audience.

When I entered the theater on my first day, all the actors were waiting in the audience for the director to arrive. Most of the other actors knew each other and were sitting together, so I found a seat by myself and settled in for twenty minutes of nervous waiting.

When the director finally showed up, he and his three assistants promptly sat down at the back of the audience and he began barking out orders over a microphone. This director was all business, and we started blocking the first scene right away.

He informed us that the actors with lines had already spent two weeks in line rehearsal, so we would move along very quickly.

When we reached the first scene in which I appeared, the director told us all to take our places. This scene took place in some kind of hospital. While I wasn't exactly sure what kind of hospital, I assumed that the director was going to explain everything to us. I got up onstage with my fellow actors and I stood to the side, not having any idea where to go.

In a booming voice, the director yelled "Action!" All the actors but me started moving onstage and talking in character, as I continued to stand in my spot waiting for the director's instructions. Suddenly, the director started yelling at someone onstage.

"Hey, retard, don't you know what you're doing?"

I looked around to see what poor soul he was yelling at. To my horror, I realized that everybody onstage had stopped, and all eyes were on me.

I slowly looked at the director and meekly said, "Me?"

"Yeah," he replied in a not-so-kind voice. "I'm talking to you, idiot. I don't have time for you to screw around in my theater. You are a frontal lobotomy patient, so for God's sake, be one!" And then after what seemed like a few excruciating minutes, he said "Go!" Everyone else began acting once again while I just stared at him, not having any idea what I was supposed to do. I didn't think he was doing a very good job of directing me, because he still hadn't told me what to do.

"Stop!" This time he came onto the stage and walked right up to me. Looking me directly in the eyes, he asked, "Do you know what a frontal lobotomy is?" I didn't answer him, because I had no clue. "You don't know!?" He spun on his heels and started to head back into the audience. After a few steps, when he realized that I was still standing there, he turned and yelled, "Get out! You're fired!"

On the bus ride back home, I had a chance to think about what had just happened. I was fired from my first professional acting job because... well, honestly, I had no idea why.

When I got off the bus, I had to walk through my old high school campus to get home. I passed by the theater, and without thinking about it I went to Mr. Coffey's office. He was still there even though it was late in the evening. I stood outside of his office, not sure why I was there, because I didn't want him to know what had happened. Just when I was about to leave, he noticed me and invited me in.

"How did it go?" he asked. His excitement was palpable. "You're back early. Is everything okay?"

I broke down and told him the whole story. When I was done, I confessed that I had no idea why I was fired. Mr. Coffey looked confused, and at first I thought that he didn't know why I had been fired either. Then he spoke slowly, in a controlled voice. "Scott, you were not prepared. You did no research on the play or your character, and you made me look bad because I recommended you for the part."

I didn't understand what he was talking about. I had no lines, what was there to research or prepare for? I told him that, because my part was so small, I thought the director would tell me what to do.

"There are no small parts," he said, "only small actors."

"Small?" I thought. *"I'm six feet tall."*

Sitting me down, he said, "You did not take this job seriously. The first thing you must do is know the show forward and backwards. Then you must know your character, so you can *become* your character. Your job as an actor is to make sure the audience believes you *are* the character, not just pretending to be the character. You must believe before the audience can believe."

Mr. Coffey paused, and his mood darkened. "Scott, you can go through life waiting for people to tell you what to do, or you can be prepared for life, so you can show them who you are. Going through life with blinders on is not living at all. You've got to take chances in life, but it's up to you." We looked at each other for a few very awkward moments. Then he said he had work to get back to and wished me luck.

As I walked home, I kept thinking about what he had said: *There are no small parts, only small actors.* The next morning, I went to the local library and found Miss Robinson who had helped me out with my audition monologue the year before. I told her what had happened and asked her if she had heard of the play *One Flew Over the Cuckoo's Nest,* and if she knew what a frontal lobotomy patient was. I felt comfortable talking to this woman, and I trusted that she would be kind and honest with me.

We spent the next two hours talking. She described the outline of the play to me, and explained what a frontal lobotomy was. She even showed me pictures of patients who had undergone the procedure.

"Wow; I had no idea that if a person was too violent, one way to control them was to perform an operation on their brain, turning them into a docile vegetable. How barbaric! Do you have any more books on this inhumane and archaic practice?" I asked.

"Yes, I do," she assured me. "But if you really want to know more, I think you should visit the Mental Hospital in Napa."

"What? I thought all of this stuff was no longer in existence in 1974." She assured me that it was still all too real, and gave me the information I needed to get to the hospital and see for myself.

One week later, under the cover story of working on a paper for a college project, I was standing in the middle of a real mental ward. I stood very still, listening and watching everything, taking in all the sounds, smells, and feelings I was experiencing. After about an hour of just absorbing my surroundings, I asked an orderly if there were any frontal lobotomy patients in this ward. The orderly told me that there were, but that I should be prepared for what I was about to see.

I slowly followed him down a hallway that led to a door with a small window. He told me that I could look if I wanted, that the patient would not mind, and then he left. All alone, I timidly peered into the small window, and what I saw shocked me to the core.

In the middle of a small room that had padding on the walls and floor, a patient was wearing a straitjacket. His head had been unevenly shaved, exposing a three-inch scar on his forehead, and he was drooling and making random sounds and movements. Transfixed, I started writing down everything I was witnessing. Despite how uncomfortable it felt to watch this poor man, I realized he was still a human being.

When I left the hospital, I finally understood what my teacher meant by *no small part*. My job playing a frontal lobotomy patient was to show an audience what it really meant to be in a mental institution in our country at that time.

The next day I went back to the library to show Miss Robinson all the notes that I had taken, and shared with her what I had seen and learned at the hospital.

"So, Scott, what do you plan on doing with all this new-found knowledge?" she asked.

"I don't know," I replied.

"Why not go back to the theater and show the director what you've learned?"

"I'm not sure that's a good idea. The director was really angry with me, and he probably gave my part to someone else."

"The point is not to get your part back, but to show the director that you finally understand what it means to be an actor," she stated.

"You really think that's a good idea?"

"I do."

I left the library thinking about what she had said. In the end I decided that she was right, and got on the first bus to San Francisco.

When I arrived at the theater, I asked the stage manager if I could talk with the director. He told me that he was very busy because the play was opening in a couple of days, but that he would tell the director I was there and that I could wait for him in the theater. I thanked him, went in, and sat down in the audience. There was a rehearsal going on, so I observed the actors as they practiced.

About an hour later, the director came over and very impatiently asked me what I wanted. I told him that I had figured out why he had fired me, and that I now knew what a frontal lobotomy patient was.

"You interrupted my rehearsal to tell me that?" he asked testily.

I nodded meekly and got up to go.

"Hold on," he snapped. "Don't tell me; show me." And he pointed to the stage.

I was confused. What did he want me to do?

"Get up on my stage and *show* me that you are a frontal lobotomy patient." And with that, he instructed the rest of the actors to start from the top of the scene.

I was still reeling from this sudden turnabout, but when I stepped onto the stage a funny thing happened to me: I didn't go up there as Scott *the actor*, but as Scott *the frontal lobotomy patient*. Because of my research trip to the hospital, I knew just what to do. Drool and spittle sprayed the audience as I convulsed and seized on stage.

"Aaahh, woff woff, bua bua," I blurted out in a contorted voice.

I was not pretending to be a frontal lobotomy patient; I *was* a frontal lobotomy patient. As the scene continued and actors passed me onstage, I reacted to them not as an actor but as my character. I was not acting, I was reacting. I didn't have any lines, but I was a patient in this hospital ward, and the other actors treated me like one.

When the scene was over, I came down from the stage and started walking out through the audience, satisfied that I had learned what it meant to be an actor.

"Hold on there," said the director. "Where are you going? Wardrobe is the other way."

I was rehired, and for two hours at a time, eight shows per week, I was somebody else. By the end of the first week, I had developed a whole backstory and history for this man who I was playing.

One night after the show, having changed back into my street clothes, I was leaving the theater through the lobby at the same time as an older woman who had been in the audience. When she saw me, she went to the big metal and glass exit doors and opened one for me, then held it until I went through. I thanked her, though I wasn't sure why she would hold the heavy door for me when I should have been the one holding it for her. Then, when we were out of the theater and onto the sidewalk, she asked if she could call me a cab. Again I wondered why—and then it hit me: This woman actually thought I *was* a frontal lobotomy patient, and incapable of doing these things for myself.

I had done it. I believed I was the character, and so did she. Mr. Coffey was right: there were no small parts. I had become an actor.

Just as I finished sharing my story, Miss Gates, one of the school's administrators, came into the multi-purpose room. She announced that the bus had arrived, and it was time for us to leave for the theater.

Once all the kids were safely seated on the bus, I moved to the front where I could sit by myself. I was mentally exhausted from having just relived so many memories, and a peaceful hour-long bus ride sounded great. As I looked out the bus window and gazed at the scenery passing by, my mind began to drift, and I started to relax. Then a tap on my shoulder brought me back to the present.

"Can I sit up here with you, Mr. D?" Grace asked. "I have a question about the play, and I don't want anyone else to hear."

With all the noise the kids were making and the rumbling of the bus, I was sure that no one could overhear us, so I reluctantly moved over. As soon as Grace sat down next to me, she immediately started in.

*"I **am** really nervous about the play, Mr. D, but that's not what I wanted to talk to you about." She paused and took a deep breath. "Before I came to Armstrong in the fourth grade, I had a really hard*

time in school and at home." Looking away, Grace continued tentatively, "I had no hope, or even a reason for going on, and umm... I
tried to hurt myself... if you know what I mean.

"What I'm worried about, Mr. D, is what's going to happen to
me when I go back to my old school district. I start high school in the
fall, and as much as I would love to continue acting, I know I won't.
I know I'm going to have a real hard time just trying to keep my
grades up even without doing any extracurricular activities. That
means no drama, no basketball, just studying. But that's not what
I'm really afraid of..." She fell silent, trying to fight back tears.

After a few moments, I chimed in with my two cents. "It's okay
to be scared, Grace; we're all afraid to fail in a new schoo—"

"I'm not afraid to fail, Mr. D; I'm afraid to **die**," she interrupted.
"I'm terrified I'll fall back down that rabbit hole of depression like I
did before... but that this time, maybe I will... you know... maybe I'll
really do it... this time."

Tears slid down her face while I gently put my arm around her
shoulder. "Let me share something else with you, Grace."

17.

SUICIDE IS NOT PAINLESS

I had just flunked out of Cal. I had no idea what I was going to do with myself, and my life had no direction. Despite my mother's influence, I felt completely alone, both hapless and hopeless. I was tired of beating my head against the wall. Flunking out of Cal proved to me that all those teachers and kids who once said I was useless and would never amount to anything had been right. What was the point of going on? I felt this way for a couple of months, and no matter how hard I tried to find some hope in my life, I found nothing.

One afternoon while driving through the Oakland Hills, I suddenly realized that all it would take to relieve me of my despair would be one sharp swerve. I could drive right off the cliff. That would be it: no more problems, no more disappointing the people in my life, no more trying to fit in. I would be free, and all it would take would be one yank of the wheel.

I was approaching the highest peak in the hills on a straightaway before a very sharp turn. This was the perfect place. So, determined to drive off the cliff ahead, I picked up speed. For some reason, I wasn't scared. I felt relieved. I thought that I had finally found a solution to take away all of my pain. I truly didn't think that anyone, not even my mother, would miss me. I know how self-centered that sounds, but in that moment I was so down on myself, so damaged, that I truly thought the world would be better off without me in it.

Right before I crested the peak of the hill, just moments before I was going to make a sharp turn and drive off the cliff, I felt a cold, wet nose on my neck. I froze.

It was Annie, our family dog, and she was licking my neck. I had totally forgotten that she was in the car with me. I immediately pulled over. I was sobbing, and she was licking the tears off my face. Annie had saved my life, but I still didn't believe it was a life worth saving.

I sat in the car feeling like a total failure, because I couldn't even do *this* right. I couldn't hide from my problems, and I couldn't solve them either. I was in limbo. It seemed like I was slowly sinking in quicksand, with nothing and nobody to help me. I didn't believe anyone understood what I was going through or who I was. I felt completely and utterly alone. For some reason, it was very important to me to make people believe everything was fine, and that flunking out of Cal didn't bother me. I don't know why, but I wanted to look like I was doing well to everyone else on the outside, even though nothing seemed well at all to myself on the inside.

In the days after my "suicide attempt" was thwarted by a canine, I stopped running, acting, and playing the drums. Historically, these activities had made me feel good about myself. I think that, deep down inside, I felt I didn't deserve anything good. I lived at home and worked in a deli. I was twenty-three years old, but could have been sixty. Mentally, I had stopped growing and had no interest in changing my circumstances. I believed I deserved to be where I was, and I had no intention of changing because I saw no point. I had tried coming out of the Shadows, and I had gotten what I deserved for it. So back into the Shadows I went, and the Shadows were where I planned to stay.

"It's always darkest before the dawn." My parents quoted this frequently. I had no idea what it meant, nor did I care. I always took these kinds of sayings very literally: Of course it's dark before the sun comes up, duh. My parents often said crazy things that made no sense to me. "Just put one foot in front of the other." Okay.

Now, I'm sure these metaphors meant something to my parents, but they didn't mean anything to me. About eighteen years later, I co-wrote a musical called *Heaven in '57*. The main song, "BELIEVE," contained these lyrics:

> *When there's something you dream about*
> *When there's something you need*
> *There is always some hope about*
> *Right here—if you believe*
> *It may not be clear to you*
> *How near it is, but see*
> *Inside there's your miracle*
> *In your heart lies your happiness*
> *All you need now, you do possess*
> *If only you*
> *Believe*

Still trying to control her emotions, Grace said, "Mr. D, I had no idea. You seem like you have it all together." A moment of silence passed while she composed herself. "I sang that song for my audition for this year's play. You gave it to me. I had no idea you wrote that song, or what it meant to you."

"Grace," I said, "'if only you believe' are the hardest words to follow." Grace nodded. "To believe in yourself, without actual proof that everything will be okay, is terrifying. It's blind faith, and that's hard to have when you're full of self-doubt."

"So how did you do it, Mr. D? How did you get through this?"

18.

On My Way to My Great Demise

A funny thing happened on the way to my Great Demise: I got hope again, and it was quite by accident.

One day, on my way home from work, I was walking through my old junior high. It was after school, but there were a bunch of kids out by the track. I wasn't sure what was going on, so I went down to look. Mr. Ball was standing in the middle of the kids and giving them instructions about a run they were about to take. I didn't want him to notice me, because I didn't want to explain why I was no longer at Cal. But no sooner had I started to walk away than I heard him shout, "Hey, Scott, come here!"

To my horror, he proceeded to introduce me to the group of junior high runners. "Gentlemen, it is my great honor and privilege to introduce to you a local track star and alumni of this school, Scott Douthit." *Crap.* I had to get away, but it was too late. The runners surrounded me and started giving me high fives, bombarding me with questions about running.

"How old were you when you started running?"

"How many miles do you run a day?"

"What's your favorite distance?"

Everything started closing in on me, and all I wanted was to get away and hide, but there was nowhere for me to go. After a few excruciating minutes of attempting to answer their questions, Mr. Ball realized I was struggling with the attention and sent the kids for a warm-up jog around the track. It was time for me to escape—and then my life changed forever.

"Scott, do you want to come for a run with us?" asked Mr. Ball. "I think the kids would like it."

And there it was: *someone wanted me to help.* I know that Mr. Ball didn't see what he did that day as a big deal, but my life would never be the same.

Sometimes in life it's not the big things that make a lifelong impact, but the little ones. Running with Mr. Ball and the junior high school cross-country team made me feel important, needed, and special. It sounds corny, but all I really wanted in life was to have purpose, to make a difference, to know there was someplace where I belonged. With the small gesture of inviting me to run with his team, Mr. Ball made me feel like I had a purpose.

For the next four or five weeks, I would go over to the school to help with the team. At first I would just run with the kids, and then, slowly, I started giving pointers and advice on running styles and race strategies. Pretty soon, students started to seek me out for help and advice.

"Scott, I'm having a hard time with hill running. What do you think I should do?"

"When you get to the bottom of the hill, John, cut your speed in half, take shorter strides, and try to get up on your toes."

"You mean like sprinting?"

"Yes, but in slow motion."

"Scott, I keep getting shin splints. How do you avoid them?"

"Run heel-toe, Sam, and try not to make any noise. Don't let your foot slap the ground."

Holy smokes. Again, this sounds like such a little thing, but this opportunity showed me that there was something I could do, and that I was needed. Once the cross-country season was over, though, I assumed things would go back to normal for me. No hope for the future, just keeping my head down and staying in the Shadows.

After work one day, I decided to walk by the junior high school just to say hi. Mr. Ball and Mr. Nielson, the other PE teacher, were sitting in their office after class talking to some of the young runners. When I walked in, I got a very strange feeling. I felt comfortable, almost at home. I was treated like I was supposed to be there. A few minutes later, Mr. Ball asked me what I was doing.

I said, "I'm standing here talking to you."

"No, not right now, what are you doing for the rest of your life?"

The question stunned me. Nobody had ever asked me what my plans were for the future. I didn't have any. I must have had a confused look on my face, because then Mr. Ball asked, "Have you ever thought about going to school to be a PE teacher?"

What!? Did I hear that right? As if going back to school wasn't a ridiculous enough idea to start with, why would I go back to be a teacher? I smiled and told him that I would think about it and come by next week. Then I left, with no intentions of thinking about it or ever going back again.

What were they thinking? Didn't they know that I was too stupid for school? For some reason I was really pissed off that they would consider such a ridiculous notion. I felt completely embarrassed and helpless, again. But the strangest thing happened. The more I thought about teaching and coaching, the more attractive the idea became.

I had never had Mr. Ball or Mr. Nielson as PE teachers, but being around them now as an adult had me thinking that their jobs looked fun—but, even more importantly, worthwhile. They were making a difference in people's lives, young people's lives. There was only one problem, one fly in the ointment: going back to school.

The following week, I did go by Mr. Ball and Mr. Nielson's office. Mr. Ball asked me what I thought about his idea. I considered my answer for a moment and decided that I would be level with them. I said that I would like to be a PE teacher, but that there was no way I could go back to college.

Mr. Nielson asked me, "Why?"

Now that was a tricky question. In the past I would have run away or lied. I didn't want them to think that I was a total idiot, but I felt I needed to tell them the truth about why I couldn't go back to school. To further complicate matters, Mr. Nielson had graduated from Cal, and I didn't want to admit to him that I couldn't hack it.

In the end I explained, "I can't go back to school because my grade point average is too low. After my two quarters at Cal, my GPA was below 1.5; what college would accept me? Flunking out of Cal ruined any opportunity for me to continue in school."

Mr. Ball looked at me and asked, "What was your junior college GPA before transferring to Berkeley?"

I told them it had been pretty good. I'd had a 2.5 GPA, and my coaches had made sure that I would be eligible to run by signing me up for classes that they knew I could pass. But what difference did any of that make?

Then Mr. Ball said the wildest thing: "Don't transfer from Cal. Forget those two quarters, and transfer from your JC to start as a junior."

"What?" I asked, incredulous. "You can do that?"

"You can do whatever you want," Mr. Ball said.

I was shocked. Until that moment, I had no idea that I could still go back to school. Trying to follow this train of thought, I wondered out loud, "But where?"

Now, this is where it gets interesting. It turns out that Mr. Ball had gone to San Francisco State University, and he thought it would be a good school for me. For the next few weeks, whenever I visited his office we would talk about going back to school. I liked the idea of teaching PE, but I had no idea how to play a lot of the sports, let alone understand or explain their rules and strategies.

With great enthusiasm, Mr. Ball told me, "That's what college is for! You're not supposed to know how to do it before, only after." And according to Mr. Ball, San Francisco State was an excellent teaching school. They taught using the *Theory and Practice* method. It wasn't about the books alone; it was about learning and then performing the skills.

With help from my mom and Mr. Ball, I signed up to attend San Francisco State in the spring. I was excited, but in the back of my mind I still had doubts: Could I do this? When I got the list of classes I was scheduled to take in my first semester I was flabbergasted:

Human Anatomy
Psychology
Physiology
Kinesiology

These were my first semester classes, in a brand-new school, with a brand-new major, and I had no idea what any of these classes were about. Except for "human," I didn't even know what the other words meant, and there were way too many *–ologies*. I was doomed.

I knew that I was going to fail at this new school like I had always failed at anything school-related, but I attended anyway. My first day in anatomy class scared me to death. My mom bought me a book called *Gray's Anatomy.* This book contained a lot of pictures, which I liked, but something was off—the pictures were mostly of bones and muscles and the skeletal system. I thought my mom had made a mistake. This book was for doctors and nurses, not for soon-to-be PE teachers. Why would I have to learn anything like this? I couldn't foresee a time when I would ever need this type of information.

When I got to the lecture, a lot of the students in the classroom were nursing majors. I was the only PE major there. When the professor began to lecture, he spoke in a low, steady tone. I didn't know what he was talking about, and it was hard to stay awake. He used words that I had never heard before, like "supination» and "pronation." When the lecture was finally over, I was in a complete panic. I was going down in flames... again.

As I walked out of the lecture hall, I asked one of the other students, "How are we supposed to remember all of this?"

"I hear the lab will explain it all," she replied.

"What lab?" I asked.

"Human Anatomy. It's our next class and it's in ten minutes." I must have looked utterly confused because she gently took hold of my arm. "You're going the wrong way. Come with me, and I'll show you where it is."

Great, now I had to go, but I assured myself that this would be the only time I would attend; as soon as the lab was over, I'd be out of there. I was about to discover that Human Anatomy was the study of the human body, and that the human anatomy lab was where you got to see and touch the human body. Unfortunately, the human body that I was supposed to touch would be dead.

The anatomy science lab was very large, with tables that could hold four students per work station. The lab was very clean and sterile looking, except for two skeletons hanging from supports on either side of the room. I walked into this odd-looking space and tentatively sat down at the first open table. Once I'd settled in, I started scanning the area for more signs and hints of what I had to look forward to in this class.

The far wall was adorned with pictures of the human body. Underneath the windows, rows of small boxes contained a variety of bones waiting for someone to pull them out and examine them. But what caught my attention more than any of the other objects was a plate glass sliding door on the other side of the classroom. This door led to another room, but the lights were out on the other side of the glass.

Unfortunately, my curiosity got the best of me. So, while the rest of the class was waiting for the teacher to arrive, I left my desk and entered the darkened room. I was reluctant to turn on the lights for fear of getting in trouble, so I peered around the dimly lit area trying to determine what was inside.

This room was about the same size as the other one I had just left, but there were no desks. Instead, six long shapes that appeared to be rolling beds sat in the center of the room. I pressed forward, intrigued. As I approached the first bed, I realized it was a metal gurney—with a naked human body laying prone atop it. My imagination went wild with visions of zombies. What was this place?

I rushed out of the room, returned to my desk as fast as I could, and asked one of my classmates if they knew that there was a room full of dead people next door. One of the nursing majors matter-of-factly informed me that they were not called "dead bodies" but "cadavers." And they were *our* cadavers. Great! I didn't know what cadavers were used for, and I was pretty sure I didn't want to find out.

Forget waiting for class to be over; I was ready to bolt *now*. But just then, the door of the lab opened, and in walked this beautiful woman about my own age dressed in a bathrobe. It looked like I wasn't the only one who was in the wrong place. Instead of sitting down at one of the tables, though, she walked up to the front of the classroom, faced us, and introduced herself as our TA for the semester.

By this time, I was starting to realize that these people really were serious. This was a real science course. I couldn't wait to escape this loony bin with skeletons and bones and dead bodies, and I decided that as soon as there was a break, I was out of there. Then our TA said something that would change the course of my academic career forever. She said that we had to learn the names of all the major muscle groups in the human body by the end of the three-hour lab.

I knew there was no way that I was going to learn the names of *all* the muscles in my body by the end of this class, or ever. I guess the TA could see the doubt on my face. She walked over to me and said, in front of the whole class, "You look skeptical, but I guarantee you will learn the muscle groups before you leave class today; trust me."

And then it happened. This beautiful TA climbed up onto my lab table and took off her bathrobe. What was she doing? There she was, standing in front of the entire class in a bikini. What on earth was she thinking? (Not that I had any complaints.)

"Class," she said, looking directly at me, "you have my permission to stare at my body for as long as you want." What kind of school was this? Like many others in the room, I was in fact taking the TA up on her offer—only not for the reason you might suppose, but because she had painted her skin to indicate each muscle group. Her biceps were red, and her triceps were blue.

I couldn't believe it. I could see where each muscle group started and ended on her body. She instructed us to touch and feel our own muscles. What? This must be a trick. Where was the lecture with pages and pages of text that didn't mean anything? Here I was, staring at a beautiful woman's legs and realizing that I was seeing her quadriceps and hamstrings and calf muscles. And to my astonishment, she was right: by the end of that class I *had* learned all of the major muscle groups.

The following week it was time for us to dissect a cadaver, and I got hands-on experience with muscles and bones and ligaments and tendons. For the first time in my life, I was learning because I was able to touch and feel and pull and tug. I was using my hands and it was okay.

My TA told me that she'd concluded I was a kinesthetic learner, and that this class would be perfect for me because I learned by touch and feel. Again, I couldn't believe it. Not only was she sure I could learn, but she also assured me that I would do well in this class. This was when I found out I had a learning *style*, and I was hooked.

I don't want to make it sound like out of the blue, the skies opened, and everything in school made sense. That was not the case. But I discovered that if I looked at a problem *in the right way*, I could figure it out. I was a hands-on learner, and for the first time in my long history of educational intimidation I started to develop confidence in myself, confidence that I could eventually figure things out. Even more significantly, though, I started feeling that I belonged in school. I just had to adapt.

Consider: Exercise Physiology, the study of your body in motion. There were two parts to this class. The first part required the students to do experiments and the second part required us to record the outcome of the experiments by writing the results in a journal. We would work in teams of four to five, each with our own jobs. In Physiology Lab we experimented on animals, but in Exercise Physiology Lab we experimented on each other. Nobody else wanted to be the guinea pig, and I didn't want to be responsible for recording the results, since I was still very bad at taking notes and spelling. So I gladly volunteered to be the guinea pig for every one of our experiments.

In our first experiment, we monitored the effects of hot and cold water on heart rate. As a group, we had to make an educated guess about what would happen when the victim (or rather, volunteer) was immersed in either freezing water or very hot water. So, before we conducted the experiment, we discussed what we thought would happen if, for example, the subject was sitting in a whirlpool of ice water. Would his heart rate increase or decrease—and either way, why? This is where things started to really click for me, because I was able to visualize *what* was going to happen. And, perhaps even more importantly, I would try to imagine *why* it was going to happen.

In the case of cold immersion, everyone in my group thought that the subject's heart rate (the "subject," in this case, being me) would go up and stay up. My resting heart rate was about 55 beats per minute, and they expected it would easily go up to anywhere between 170 and 190 beats per minute during the experiment. Because this was going to physically happen to me, I was able to use my imagination and preview what would be occurring to my body while I sat in the freezing water. At the outset, I was the only one in my group who thought that my heart rate would go up at first, but then drop back down to under 100.

Our group leader, a female student, asked me why I had reached that conclusion. In the past this question would have made me change my mind, because I would have assumed that she must be smarter than me. But for the first time I started to think independently, and with some confidence.

In my head I could not imagine my heart rate remaining at 180 for very long; my heart would have to slow down, or it would explode. I figured that my body would shut down all unnecessary functions and try to slow down as much as possible. I expected my group to laugh at my answer, but instead our group leader said, "Interesting thesis. Let's find out who's right." My answer was not dismissed, and all our hypotheses were going to be put to the test.

Our group went to our athletic training room and hooked me up to a heart monitor and blood pressure cuff. When I was ready, I got into a small metal tub and sat down wearing just my running shorts. Then my team filled the tub with cold water... and four bags of ice cubes.

My heart rate shot straight up to over 200 beats per minute. I found it hard to breathe, and I was questioning my strategy of volunteering to be the guinea pig. But after about a minute and a half my heart rate started dropping, and after five minutes my heart rate was under 100. My guess had been correct: In the extreme cold, your heart rate will eventually drop because the body is trying to protect itself.

I was also right about the fact that the body shuts down all unnecessary functions. I had eaten about twenty minutes before the test began, and when I was finished I could tell that I still had undigested food in my stomach. My body had stopped digesting the food as it attempted to deal with the extreme cold.

Over the next few years, I became my own student. I realized that I didn't learn the same way that other students did. Reading a book or listening to a lecture was not going to cut it for me, so I started thinking outside the box. I began using the part of my brain that I knew worked well: my imagination. When my history professor lectured about the Battle of Bunker Hill, I asked a few of my classmates to join me in the woods for a reenactment of the battle.

"Charge!" yelled the British commander, as his troops surged forward.

"They fell for our trap!" yelled a colonial soldier. "We'll make them pay for being arrogant Brits!" The battle raged on until we had acted out the entire lecture.

When studying reproduction in my Human Sexuality class, some of my classmates joined me in recreating the cellular process at a larger scale. A few people made a circle holding hands, desperately trying to keep the swimming sperm from reaching their destination. We all had a great time, and I was able to comprehend the information. I started to fit in at school. I was still that weird guy, but now I was that weird guy with cool ideas.

I started to worry less and less about what other people thought of me, and concerned myself more with what I thought of myself. For the first time in my life, I started to develop confidence in my own abilities—confidence in abilities that I just had not imagined I had. I was starting to really enjoy life and who I was becoming. I had never seen myself as being academically successful before, but I was becoming successful now. I was getting good grades, understanding and enjoying my classes, and meeting new people. In fact, I met my wife Lynn at SF State. This was a new me, and I liked it.

"I thought I knew your story, Mr. D, but I didn't. Not even close. Thank you for sharing. It really means a lot to me."

After a few moments of silence, Grace continued, "Well, at least when you became a teacher everything fit into place. You're such an amazing teacher and role model to us. I'm so glad you found teaching. At least something finally started to come easy for you." She looked at me hopefully. "No more hurdles for you to get over, right?"

*"Life always has hurdles, Grace, but it's **how** you get over them that makes you the person you are. Being a teacher has not always been easy for me."*

19.

"ME, A TEACHER!?"

After attending San Francisco State for three years, I graduated and earned a Teaching Credential in Physical Education. Holy crap, if only those kids in elementary school could see me now. I was going to be a teacher, and not just any teacher: I was going to change the world. After graduation, I set out to be the best teacher I could be. But to me the most important thing was that I needed to teach in a public school. It was still vital to me to be legitimate, and being legitimate meant working as a public-school teacher.

Ironically, my first two years of teaching found me working in private schools. No matter how hard I tried, I simply could not find a job in the public schools. For two years I learned by trial and error, and began to develop my own teaching style and communication skills. I taught at a French American school for grades one through twelve that didn't have any PE facilities, so I had to become creative with what and where I taught. This resulted in innovations like Sprints down the hallway, Theater Combat in the parking lot, and Capture the Flag at a local park. I had to adapt, and I became very good at it. Oh, and did I mention I didn't speak French?

So, after two years of paying my dues teaching in private schools, it finally happened: I was hired to teach PE in a public elementary school.

At this point I was still very insecure about my abilities as a teacher, and I felt that the *only* way to really prove myself was to be accepted at the public-school level. In my head, I perceived a significant difference in value between public and private schools, and I did not see this difference as an opinion but as a fact. One was simply better than the other. I can't tell you how excited I was to have finally made it to what I considered to be the "Big Leagues." At last, I would make everyone proud of me. What I still hadn't realized was that the people in my life who were closest to me were already proud of me.

I was doing very well at my new school, getting great reviews and feedback from the other teachers and the principal. In fact, the principal would rave about me: "If you just stick with it, you will be the best gym teacher I've ever had." I had made it; I had arrived. I felt this way, though, not because I was making a difference in students' lives but because I had achieved what I thought of as a level of prestige and legitimacy. I wasn't proud because I was a teacher; I was proud because I was a *public-school teacher*, and nobody could take that away from me. At least, that's what I had concluded.

Three-quarters of the way through my first year at public school, my principal gave me an annual review. It was a wonderful report filled with high praise, but at the end of our meeting he asked me a simple question that would turn my world upside down. "I've been looking through your school records," he said, "but I haven't been able to find the results from your CBEST test." He smiled. "Do you know where they are? It's important that I have them in your records."

I was in shock. Not only did I not know where my CBEST results were, I didn't even know what the CBEST *was*. I had never heard of it. Seeing how nervous I was, the principal said reassuringly, "Don't worry, Scott; you were supposed to have taken the CBEST before being hired, but I'm sure it was just an oversight on the district's part. All you have to do is take the test before the end of the school year."

"I don't understand," I said. "I thought I was doing well."

"Oh, yes! You're doing very well." Smiling and nodding, he explained, "This has nothing to do with how well you're doing or how good of a teacher you are. This is just one of those hoops that you have to jump through in the course of your career." Thanking me, he shook my hand, and I was ushered out of his office.

I wasn't exactly sure what had happened. My reviews said that I was doing well as a teacher, but as it turns out, it didn't matter what my principal thought of me. The only thing that mattered to the district was whether I had passed this particular test. I'd made friends with a couple of teachers at school, and I asked them about the CBEST. "Don't worry, it's just bull; just another hoop we have to jump through." There was that saying again. What did they mean by "jumping through hoops?"

Whatever it meant, and whatever people thought about the test, I only had one way forward. After a quick check of my records, I realized that I had to take the CBEST if I wanted to continue teaching in the public schools. It was a requirement, simple as that. No problem, though; everyone was telling me the test would be a piece of cake. So I signed up for the first date available, which just so happened to be a week later at San

Francisco State. Cool—the sooner I took the test, the quicker I could get it over with and get on with my life.

I decided that I should find out what the test was all about, so I got a pamphlet that described what I could expect to encounter on it, and the topics all looked very familiar to me. Now, just because they looked familiar didn't mean that I knew them, but after the pep talk I'd gotten from my principal I felt confident that this material would magically appear in my mind when I saw the test questions. I didn't even study for the test, that's how confident I was that I would succeed.

Looking back, I'm not sure what I was basing my confidence on; maybe my success at SF State, or the confidence my principal had expressed in me. Maybe I just wanted to be like everyone else and believe this test would be a piece of cake. In any case, I went in to take the CBEST with blinders on. I was going to pass this test and continue my career—period, end of discussion.

The CBEST was given on a Saturday morning. I arrived early to walk around the campus. It was a nice morning, so I got some coffee and headed over to the building where they were administering the test. When I arrived, a long line of kids had already formed. And when I say kids, I mean *kids*. I was close to thirty by this time, and most of those standing in line were in their early twenties. Great! No problem. I had this in the bag.

I encountered the first sign of trouble when I walked into the classroom and saw chairs outfitted with tabletops. The tabletops were made for right-handers, and of course I'm left handed. I took a deep breath to calm my nerves. *"I can still do this; no problem."* I'm pretty sure those were the exact last words Custer uttered before he hastily entered history at the Little Bighorn.

The person administering the test was obviously a current student at SF State, who did not seem to be enjoying the fact that he had to be there on a Saturday morning. Handing out the test copies, he said in a bored and irritated tone, "Okay, this test is very straightforward. There are three parts: an Essay portion," *(Gee, I hope spelling won't count!)* "an English Proficiency portion," *(Say what?)* "and Rudimentary Mathematics." *(Rude-a-what?)* After explaining all the guidelines, the proctor asked, "Are there any questions?"

A student sitting next to me raised his hand and asked, "Is there a time limit?" I thought that was a silly question; why would there be a time limit for a proficiency test? What's the rush, I thought? Wasn't the goal of this test to find out whether I knew this information, not how quickly I could regurgitate it? Why would you need a time limit?

Turns out, though, it wasn't a silly question after all: yes, there was a time limit. We would have one hour for each section of the test, so three hours in total. Suddenly, all sounds stopped except for the ticking of the clock on the wall. *Tick, tock, tick, tock.* That old familiar feeling of panic started rising up my spine. Tests with time limits were always very hard for me. I forced myself to take a deep breath, told myself to relax, and started in on the Math test.

A car costs $25,000 plus $675 for tax, title, and license fees. Ari finances the car by putting down $2,500 in cash and taking out a 3-year, 4% loan. What will his monthly payments be (if figured across all 3 years rather than annually)?

Attempting to make sense of the question, I tried to organize the facts in my head. The car only cost $2,500 and I owe

$25,000 in taxes, huh? That can't be right... let me try it again. Oh, the car is $25,000 plus $675 for tax, and I put down $2,500 in cash taking out a 4-year loan at 3%... no, 3 years at 4%, oh shoot... wait, what was the question again?

The clock kept ticking. I turned to the English proficiency test, hoping it would make more sense.

In the following question, there are underlined parts to each sentence. One of the underlined parts is incorrectly written. Choose the incorrect underlined part of the sentence.

We <u>gawked at</u> him as he <u>drug</u> the picnic table <u>closer to</u> the <u>grill area</u>.

What does "gwaked" mean, and why is he on drugs? *Tick, tock, tick, tock.*

After three hours, I was done. The next week, my principal called me into his office after school and told me that he had received my results back from the CBEST. I sat down and faced him. He looked up at me and said, "You know, I really like you." Uh oh. "I think that you are a great teacher." What was he trying to tell me? And then he said it. "You did not pass the CBEST." My ears started ringing and I felt a bit sick.

"What do you mean?"

"You didn't pass all three sections. You passed the English section, but you missed passing the Essay section by two points, and the Math section by three points." I had no idea what he was talking about; I didn't know that each section was scored independently. Five points? I missed passing a three-hour test by five measly points? Couldn't he just overlook that and give me credit for passing?

"Don't worry, Scott, you only missed passing by five points; you can just take it again next month. You'll have plenty of time to study, and I'm sure that you'll do better next time." He smiled, got up from his desk, and walked over to shake my hand. As I was leaving his office, he added, "Oh, and by the way, make sure you pass it this time, because it's the last time the CBEST will be given this school year."

My head was spinning. I walked back to my desk and sat down. I wasn't sure what to think. Noticing my mood, one of my friends asked me what was wrong, and I shared what the principal had just disclosed to me. I reassured him that I would do better next time because I had only failed the test by a total of five points, but my friend looked worried.

"Well, you had better pass the CBEST next time." This was one of those moments in life that you remember with absolute clarity: what time it was, what day, what you were wearing—3:15, Friday, black sweats and a maroon shirt. "If you don't pass the CBEST by the end of this school year, they can't hire you back."

"You mean... you mean, I could be fired?"

"Yeah, didn't you know that? All teachers in the district have to pass the CBEST. I'm surprised you even got this job without already passing." There it was: pass or be fired. No pressure there.

The next two months seemed to pass in a heartbeat. I studied all the time, reviewing the mistakes I had made on the previous test. I even got books on how to pass the CBEST. I couldn't have prepared any more than I did. But here's the rub, one of the hardest parts of being dyslexic: I knew that, no matter how hard I prepared, when that clock started ticking on the wall, everything in my head would go blank. Like one of those classic Etch A Sketch toys, everything would get turned upside down and erased. I had no control over that, and the more I thought about the fact that I had to pass this test to keep my job, the worse it got.

When I sat down to take the test for the second time, I could barely read what was on the page. It didn't matter that I knew this material backwards and forwards. The only thing that mattered was that there was a time limit. No matter how hard I looked at the test page with the clock ticking in the background, I could not bring back any of that information that I had worked so hard to learn.

Needless to say, I failed the CBEST again, this time by a total of 175 points. And that was it. Because I hadn't passed the test this time, I lost my job. It was all gone. I was going the wrong way, and fast.

My whole world was once again coming down around my shoulders, and this time I wasn't alone. I was married, and my wife was pregnant with our first child. This felt like when I'd flunked out of Cal or repeated second grade. I felt like I had been exposed for whom I really was, that dummy in the back of the room who nobody liked. I'd failed, and I didn't know why. Ain't self-doubt a bitch? Everybody said that I was smart, but if I was so smart why did I just lose my job?

But the real problem was that I started to give up; I started to believe that I wasn't smart enough, good enough, or even worth the effort to *become* enough. Tests don't lie. I was still that little boy who couldn't figure out the jigsaw puzzle when everyone else could. *"Why was I so different?"* Even though I asked myself that question, truth be told, I no longer cared. I was getting what I had always known, deep down, was what I deserved.

"Wow, so why did you keep teaching?" asked Grace.

20.

SCHOOL FOR LD?

I didn't continue teaching PE for me; I continued to teach for my family. I had to support them somehow, and I felt that teaching was the only profession in which I might have a chance of doing a good job. I knew I would never teach in public schools again, though, which established for me that I would never be a legitimate teacher.

Still, I had to do something, so I got a job at a small private school in San Francisco. For the school year, teaching PE, coaching all the sports, and serving as commissioner of our athletic league, I received $12,000. Even for the early 1980s, that wasn't very much money. But what could I do? This was what I deserved.

It's funny how a test can affect your opinion of yourself, or maybe it's not so funny. All the same, my confidence was completely shaken; I felt worthless. I kept all these feelings inside, because I didn't want my family or friends, especially my wife and mother, to know how I felt about myself. I made it through the school year and then continued what had become an annual tradition: looking for a new job in the newspaper want ads.

Fortunately, thanks to glowing references from Mr. Ball and my other employers, I didn't have a problem getting job offers for the next year. This time the problem was choosing which job to take. I interviewed at a couple of schools in San Francisco that I liked, but hadn't decided on any of them yet as I headed off to the last one I had scheduled.

This final interview that I attended was for a school that taught students with LD. Now, I had no idea what LD stood for, but I figured it didn't matter because I had no intention of working at this school. It was too far away and didn't have a gym. I was just going to the interview for the experience.

There were two parts to the interview. The first required me to teach a demonstration lesson, and the second involved an interview with the principal. The campus was very beautiful, with a large athletic field.

I met the principal outside, and she told me I could go set up on the field while she brought the kids down. I decided to do a parachute lesson, because I had no idea what age range I was going to teach. Parachute lessons were usually a lot of fun. I laid the parachute out on the grass field and sat waiting there for the kids to arrive.

The classrooms were far enough away from the field that I could watch the kids approaching. They came running out to me, screaming and yelling and full of energy. They were ready to go, and so was I. For some reason I felt an unexpectedly powerful connection to these students. I had no idea why, but there was something about the way they behaved that was very familiar to me. I couldn't put my finger on it, but I felt like I knew these kids and what made them tick. No reason, just a feeling.

"Please grab the edge of the parachute and make one giant circle," I instructed. "Oops, I made a mistake. This is not a parachute... this is the ocean's surface. And if this is the surface of the ocean, can you tell me what lives in the ocean?" I asked.

"FISH!" "BARRACUDAS!" "ALGAE!" "PLANKTON!" "WHALES AND DOLPHINS!" One after another, and then all shouting at the same time, the students blurted out their answers.

Then I began to sing: "And... dunnn dunnn... dunnn dunnn... dunnn dunnn..."

The kids all screamed: "SHARK!" With a smile, I asked one of the students to slip under the parachute to play the shark, and the tag game commenced.

My parachute lesson went extremely well. In fact, it went better than it had ever gone before. Everything that I tried seemed to work, and I fed off of the kids' energy. It was like I had some kind of physical connection with these kids; it was invisible, but I could feel it all the same. I couldn't explain it, though, and it made absolutely no sense to me. I kept asking myself, *"What's different about these kids?"*

After the lesson was over, I met back up with the Principal, Jean Rime. We talked for a few minutes about how I thought I did with my lesson, and then she asked me if I had ever worked with this population before. I must have looked very confused, because she smiled and said, "Have you ever taught dyslexic students before?" Not only had I not taught dyslexics before, I had no idea what the word even meant. LD, dyslexic; what was this place?

I was ready to get out of there when Jean said to me, "You seem like a natural, like you really understand these kids, and you're the first applicant so far that they didn't destroy. Would you be interested in teaching here at Charles Armstrong

School?" I was baffled, and I didn't understand what she saw in me from just a twenty-minute lesson. I told her I would have to think about it and talk with my wife. Jean smiled, said that made sense, and that I should call her next week. I thanked her and went home, never planning to go back to that school again.

As the days passed, though, I couldn't get those kids out of my mind. What was this connection that I felt? I researched the school and discovered that "LD" stood for "learning disability," and that dyslexia was a type of learning disability. But even after my research, I still didn't fully understand what dyslexia was.

I've always wanted to make a difference, and I'd always thought that the only real place to do that would be an inner-city school whose students didn't have many resources available to them. But by the time the week was up, the draw of this school was so overwhelming that I had decided to take the job. I thought, "What the heck. It's only for a year or two, and then off to greener pastures."

My career as a PE teacher at Charles Armstrong School started in 1985, the year my son was born. I was responsible for teaching all the PE classes, covering every recess, and launching an intramural sports program. It was a very busy schedule, but it was what I was used to doing. I really didn't like sitting around doing nothing, so if I didn't have class, I was out playing with the kids at recess or on my break.

"Hey Mr. D, will you play all-time quarterback for our football game?" asked Joey.

"Sure, I'd be honored to. By the way, Joey, how's science class going?"

"Oh, so much better since you gave me the tips on how to remember pronation and supination. You're the best, Mr. D!"

It was a challenge, but it was a wonderful challenge. I was able to make personal connections with these students very quickly. I felt like I fit in, but I still didn't know why.

When I accepted the job, I didn't realize that one of my responsibilities would be to administer student screenings. Halfway through the school year, I was told that I would be giving a series of tests to students who were considering coming to school in the fall. That seemed relatively straightforward and easy, until I was told that I would need to score and evaluate the test as well.

This test was part of a screening process that our school used to evaluate the academic placement of new students. My first screening was with a second-grade girl. I was supposed to administer a series of tests to determine her processing skills, and then correct her mistakes and explain them to her while she was still there. Well, I thought to myself, how hard can a second-grade screening really be?

I remember placing five pictures on the table in front of this little girl. Each one showed the same boy in a different situation: walking his dog in the rain, eating dinner with his family, putting on his raincoat and rain boots, waking up in the morning, and drying off his wet dog. These pictures were supposed to be arranged in sequential order so that they told a story.

To my horror, I could not figure out what order to place the pictures in. I couldn't figure it out! What was wrong with me? This seemed like an easy skill, but the harder I tried the worse it got... again. I didn't know what to do, and there was no way for me to correct the girl's screening because I couldn't do it myself. I couldn't even pass a second-grade screening. Holy crap—it didn't matter where I went, stupid followed. I was caught again, and I had nowhere to hide.

Looking at those pictures, I was desperately trying to figure them out. I did not want to let this little girl know that I had no idea what I was doing. To make matters worse, Jean Rime had come into the classroom and was now looking over my shoulder. Great; not only would this little girl see that I couldn't figure it out, but so would my boss.

Sure enough, Jean asked me if she could talk to me outside. I was certain I already knew what she was going to say: "You're fired for being too stupid."

But after I followed her out the door, she smiled and asked, "Scott, are you dyslexic?"

"I didn't know dyslexia was contagious," I thought to myself. Out loud, I replied, "No, I don't think so."

Looking me straight in the eye, she said, "I recommend that you get tested to see if you are dyslexic."

Great, just what I needed: another test that I would fail.

Even at this point in my life, I still hadn't come to grips with my learning disabilities. I knew I had trouble in school, and I assumed (no matter how high an opinion my mother had of me) that I wasn't all that smart. It was easier for me to have low expectations of myself and get by than to aspire any higher and fail. Even though I was working in this school for dyslexics, I hadn't taken the time to truly understand what dyslexia was. I was just trying to get by, but Jean wouldn't let me take the easy way out. She knew that I could be something more, but I would have to push myself, and that meant figuring out what was going on in my brain.

Even though I was technically getting screened for any learning disabilities I might have, it still felt to me like I was taking a test. And to make matters worse, I was getting this "screening" at SF State, in the same building where I had previously flunked the CBEST. *Great.* I was feeling good about this... NOT.

I went to SF State the next Saturday morning. My mom came along for moral support, and stayed in the car while I went in to get screened. I felt completely alone and scared. I didn't want to be screened, because I was certain that the truth would come out: that I still wasn't good enough.

I entered the building and went to the third floor, where I found a room with a plaque on the door that read "Screening and Evaluation." Opening the door, I prepared to face my doom. The grad student sitting at the desk right inside the door looked at me and said matter-of-factly, "Take a seat; we'll get started in a few minutes." He didn't look any older than twenty; I was being tested by a *kid.* Great, this wasn't going to be embarrassing at all.

After about twenty minutes of sitting in a corner of the small office, I was ushered into a bigger room by the grad student. On one side of this new room there was a table with a chair, and on the other side four more chairs were arranged to face the seat at the table. The young grad student asked me to sit down in the lone chair, and told me that he had some students who wanted to come in and watch him give the screening as part of their class.

I was floored. I thought this was going to be private. I had had enough public humiliation to last a lifetime. The last thing I wanted was to fail in front of others, especially young college students. I wanted to run and hide and never come back. I was even contemplating changing careers. I wanted to tell this arrogant, snot-nosed grad student that he had no right to use me as a guinea pig for his class, and to take his test and *shove it.*

All this was going on inside my head, but none of it actually managed to make it out of my mouth. By the time I had truly processed what was going on, I was already sitting down in the chair. The grad student placed a series of pictures in front of me and, with a smile on his face, asked me to place them in the "proper sequence." Man eating dinner with his family, man taking a bus to work... *crap!* This was the same type of test I had administered to that second grader. While I was trying to figure out what the term "sequence" meant—I thought it meant "order," but I wasn't sure—the instructor said coldly, "You have two minutes."

My ears started ringing, my palms began to sweat, and I was having a hard time breathing. But worst of all, it became impossible to comprehend how to place those pictures in sequence. I had no idea what order to arrange them in. My eyes saw, but my brain didn't understand. And what made it worse was that I was failing a second-grade test in front of an audience. I started wondering what they must be thinking of me. Were they laughing at me, or did they just think that I was stupid?

I was still struggling with the pictures when the grad student said, "Time's up!" And with that, he picked up the pictures and put them away. Well, I thought, at least it's over and I can get out of here. But, to my dismay, he calmly put down another series of materials and said, "Here's the next part; I hope you do better." Better!? Though it might not be obvious to the average observer, I was doing my best. I had never inflicted massive bodily harm on anyone before in my life, but I was just about ready to change all that. I wanted to reach out and shove my fist so far down this guy's throat that I'd be able to tie his shoes.

I had never been so angry, but he didn't seem to notice my reaction at all. He just put the papers down on the table in front of me and said, "You have two minutes to complete this part. Go!"

And so it went for the next hour. One section after another after another, and none of them made any sense to me. I felt exactly like I did when I was in second grade and couldn't read the board, or when I was in sixth grade and couldn't spell "does," or when I was in eighth grade and couldn't climb the rope. It all came back to me: the feelings of worthlessness, inadequacy, and hopelessness.

By the time the screening had ended, I was spent. I decided that I would never subject myself to this type of misery ever again. As I got up to leave, the grad student informed me that I should come back in four days and he would personally give me my results. *"Don't do me any favors,"* I thought. *"No way am I coming back here."*

I don't remember leaving the building or walking to the street, but I somehow wound up sitting on the curb, head in my hands, weeping uncontrollably. I was completely consumed by my emotions, and couldn't stop. I don't know how she found me, but after a while I sensed that my mother was sitting next to me with her arms around me. She wasn't talking, just holding me.

Four days later, I wound up back at the same school, in the same office, with the same young grad student. We sat facing each other at his desk. He had a printout of the results from my screening, and he was trying to explain them to me, but it was like he was speaking a foreign language. I had no idea what he was saying, and for that matter, I didn't care what he had to say. I was still mad at him. It's been more than thirty years since that grad student read my results to me, but I remember the moment as if it were yesterday.

In a very official sounding voice he read, "Your diagnosis is that you have a language processing disorder, auditory processing difficulties, and expressive language disabilities. You seem to have a desire and passion for working as a teacher, but you do not have the aptitude for college or a college career." He also informed me that I was in fact dyslexic, and joked that I "should be the poster boy for dyslexia." Then he recommended that I should take vocational training, thanked me for coming, and left the room.

I sat there in complete shock, without any idea of what to do or where to go. It had finally happened: the real world had caught up with me and exposed me for who I really was. I was a nobody, a nothing, just dumb old Scotty.

I wound up back in my car sitting next to my mother, with a piece of paper in my hand that defined me. My mother asked if she could read the results. Why not? It didn't matter anymore. I had been found out and exposed. I wasn't sure what being visual and auditory dyslexic meant, but I knew what the word "disability" meant, or at least I thought I did, and it wasn't good.

"Don't have the aptitude for college? You've already graduated college," my mom hissed. As she frowned at the page, her face turned tomato red, with veins throbbing—veins I never knew existed in a human head, let alone my mom's. Her muscles tensed as she gripped the results, strangling the life out of the printed paper like a hungry hawk clasping its knife-like talons on a whimpering field mouse. Mom looked at the results, glared at the "professional's" name on the bottom of the page, and scanned the paper down and up, up and down. Her glossy eyes fixed on the results, looked at me, then twisted the paper into a corkscrew and slammed it down to the floor of the car where her black shoes trembled.

For the first time in my life, my mother's actions shocked me speechless. I didn't know what to think about what I had just witnessed, so I sat next to her in silence. Afraid to ask a question, but equally afraid to hear her response. In the end, instead of driving off, we got out of the car and went for a walk while we talked. She tried to explain to me that this was good news; that after all those years of being told I was stupid and not good enough, these results concluded that I could learn, just differently.

I ultimately decided that I wasn't going to let this random person tell me who I was or what I was worth. But there was still a bigger problem: I had to give these results to my principal, and I was certain that the same thing which happened after I flunked the CBEST would happen again after she read these results. Goodbye teaching career, hello Shadows. Only this time, I was going to stay in the Shadows and never come back out. It was just too painful to keep trying. I would get a simple job, one where I wouldn't have to keep putting myself out there for people to judge me.

I couldn't wait to get it over with, to let the truth be known and take my medicine like I deserved. The very next day, I had an appointment with Principal Jean Rime to review the results from my screening. I walked into her office and she greeted me with a beaming smile. She thanked me for getting the screening done so quickly, and began reading over the results in silence while I sat there, resolute and prepared for the worst. I had already decided I was going to be fired, but it was okay; I didn't deserve to be a teacher. There was something wrong with me, something wrong with my brain which I needed to figure out. I wasn't mad at Jean, because it was her job to do what was best for the children in her care.

After a few minutes, Jean put the paper down, looked directly into my eyes, and smiled again. Then she said something

I had not expected to hear, ever: "Welcome home, Scott; welcome home."

And she was right; I finally had come home. At this school, I had discovered something I'd been searching for my whole life, and almost given up on finding outside my family: Someplace where I could make a positive difference in people's lives. Someplace where my weaknesses would become my strengths.

"I always wondered how we were so lucky to get you as our teacher, Mr. D. Now I know," said Grace quietly.

The bus finally arrived at the theater, and Grace joined her classmates as the cast of Annie *disembarked. Surging into the building, the actors went backstage to start preparing for the show.*

I'd had no idea that I would be sharing my life story today, and I was relieved and ready to start preparing for opening night— alone. I spent the next hour doing my normal pre-show routine: making sure I had a roll of duct tape, hair brush, and pocket mirror in case of costume or make-up mishaps, checking the props to make sure they were all in order, and going over the script one last time.

Ten minutes to curtain, I went backstage to the dressing room to give the kids my annual pre-show pep talk. The energy level was through the roof, and the kids were nervously chatting until they saw me enter. I made my way to the center of the room and stood up on an empty chair.

"All right, this is it!" I said as loud as I could, so the entire cast could hear me. "Are you ready!?" The room erupted with hoots and hollers. I continued, "You've all worked very hard these last three months with all the extra rehearsals and late practices. I am so proud of all of you. Now this is the payoff—tonight is all about you. Have

fun and enjoy it!" A big cheer went up, just before the stage manager came in and told everyone that it was time to take their places.

I had taken my usual position on the left side of the wings of the stage as the curtain went up on our production of Annie. My only job during the show was solving any of the unforeseen problems that could occur during live theater, or "putting out fires" as the stage manager liked to say. As the overture began, I waited for the actors to join me in the wings. Suddenly, Grace was right beside me, squeezing my arm in a vice-like grip.

"Are you all right, Grace?" I asked.

"No! No, I am not okay. I can't remember my lines, Mr. D." Her panic was very real and very present. "Everything is blank!" She punctuated this with a sob. "What do I do? What if I go onstage and can't remember my lines? I'll look so stupid in front of five hundred people." Terrified, Grace turned to leave. "I don't think I can do this, Mr. D; I just can't go onstage!" she declared.

I gently put my hand on her shoulder. Grace turned and faced me. Her eyes were red, tears were running down her cheeks, and she wore a panicked expression. In that moment, I realized that what I said in the next few seconds would affect her for the rest of her life. I put my second hand on her other shoulder and got as close as I could so she could hear me over the music onstage.

"You are going to be fine!"

"How do you know, Mr. D?"

"I would not have cast you as Annie if I didn't think you could do it. You must have faith in yourself, Grace. Trust that you can do this. I believe in you, but it really doesn't matter what I think, because there's only one person in this world who needs to believe in you."

Grace now looked scared and confused. "One person?" she asked anxiously. "Who?"

Calling on my flair for the dramatic, I pulled the small mirror out of my pocket and angled it at her face, so she could see her own reflection.

"What are you doing, Mr. D? Is there something wrong with my makeup?"

I shook my head, and continued to hold the mirror up before her. "Just one person must believe in you, Grace. Just one."

As she stared at herself in the mirror, I watched the "Eureka!" moment spread across her face. Just then, the stage manager interrupted our conversation, cueing Grace to go onstage. And with that, she was gone.

I closed my eyes and waited. Was I right, or had I just sent that girl out to face certain humiliation that might scar her for life? I listened, holding my breath.

"I want my mommy and daddy," cried Molly.

"Molly, we ain't got mommies and daddies, and we ain't ever gonna have them. That's why we're called orphans," Pepper affirmed.

Okay, Grace, you can do this, I thought to myself with my eyes still shut. There was a pause out on stage. "Oh no..." I whispered. But then—

"I'm not an orphan! My parents are alive, and they're coming to get me, someday!"

I took a deep breath, opened my eyes, and watched the play gather steam as Grace launched into a brilliant performance as Annie.

After a successful show, climaxing in a standing ovation, the cast took their final bow and the curtain closed. All the actors were jumping, hugging, and cheering, hardly able to contain their excitement. They knew they had done their best, and I couldn't have been prouder of them. As the cast excitedly headed out into the lobby to greet their fans, I stayed behind to help the stage manager set up for the next night's show.

Feeling a tap on my shoulder, I turned around. It was Grace. She was shaking with excitement.

"You did it, Grace! You were amazing. I am so prou—"

Grace, no longer able to control her emotions, interrupted me. "Now I understand what you were trying to tell me. Why you had me look into the mirror." Then she hugged me, fiercely. "Thank you," she said into my coat, her voice muffled and thick with tears. "Thank you."

It was in that moment that I realized I did matter. That every single struggle I have encountered throughout my life has helped shape me into the person I am today. I can finally say that I am proud and happy with who I am and what I have accomplished. I am a teacher, an actor, a writer, a brother, a father, a son, a husband—and, oh yeah, a dyslexic. None of these things define me, but every one of them is a valuable part of who I am.

ABOUT THE AUTHOR

Scott Douthit was born in Fairbanks, Alaska, and grew up in Berkeley, California, where he discovered the joy of acting in high school. Crossing the bay, he graduated from San Francisco State University and earned his teaching credential, which has since been put to good use at Charles Armstrong School in Belmont, California. Mr. Douthit's passion for the stage and his creative teaching style have energized and engaged Armstrong students for more than thirty-five years. As a proud dyslexic learner himself, he shares Armstrong's mission to empower and unlock the unique potential of those with dyslexia and other learning differences. Today Scott lives in South San Francisco, where he and the love of his life were married and raised their two amazing children.

You may reach Scott via his website:
www.mydyslexiclife.com

RESOURCES

Here are some resources for parents to learn more about how to navigate their children's learning differences.

Understood: www.understood.org

National Center for Learning Disabilities: www.ncld.org

International Dyslexia Association: www.dyslexiaida.org

Great Schools Network: www.greatschoolsnetwork.org

Learning Ally: www.learningally.org

Parents Helping Parents: www.php.com

Decoding Dyslexia: www.decodingdyslexia.net

Parents Education Network: www.parentseducationnetwork.org